On Following the Dots

about a sojourn in Barcelona,
a breakdown in Baltimore, and
finding your path,
no matter where you are

Delshan Tyette Baker

Forward by Naeem

On Following the Dots is a work of nonfiction. Some names, identifying details, and specifics have been changed to protect privacy and/or anonymity. For real names, identifying details, and specifics used, they are used both with permission and with extreme gratitude.

Copyright © 2020 by Delshan Baker

Internal photo is courtesy of the author.
Cover photo by Shamerrah Parrison.

Cover design by Cruz Caldera Creative and Delshan Tyette Art.

Library of Congress Control Number: 2020908482

Published by Endeavor TBD in Baltimore, MD

ISBN-978-1-7349034-0-9 (paperback)
ISBN-978-1-7349034-1-6 (e-book)

To my father, friend and forever fan, Ellwood Hanks.
He said to make known why this is important.
This is important because it is for you.

IN GRATITUDE

To James Baldwin, for the sacrifice of sadness he made to be a witness.

ADVISEMENTS

On Medical and Mental Health

I am not a medical or mental health professional, and this book is not meant to provide medical or mental health advice. The intent is to offer opinions and options around interpreting and reacting to the many occurrences that may happen in our lives. This publication is meant as a source of valuable information for the reader; however, it is not meant as a substitute for the attention and care of a medical and/or mental health professional. If you find yourself in need, please seek out medical or mental health attention; it is more than okay.

On the Deaths of People at the Hands of Other People

Where I recount the stories of deaths of real people at the hands of other real people, both information and opinions are included. The details reflect public facing information from multiple news sources and are alleged. The opinions are exactly that: opinions; albeit, they are strong ones.

On God and the Universe

I believe. I sometimes describe myself as a spiritualist, sometimes as a heathen in Catholic girls' clothing, and most often as a soul in a body having a human experience. I do believe in that which is bigger and greater than ourselves, and in forces of good that steward this plane of existence. And mostly, I believe in trying to be a good person — doing unto others as you would have them do unto you and loving your neighbor as you love yourself. I make mention of God and the Universe, in line with my own beliefs. If this throws you, feel free to read God as Good and the Universe as That Which Unites Us. The Universe is far too old to care what we call her, and I would posit that it matters less to God how many o's it takes us to find Good, than it does that Good is found.

ACKNOWLEDGMENTS

It is impossible to name the countless loved ones, supporters, advisors, and influential strangers who have been instrumental in making this work a reality. Through your perfectly timed words, probing questions, generous refuge, and joy, you were there and are here on the journey with me. Thank you.

Here I'd like to acknowledge a few people, in particular, who without their direct contributions and guidance, this book would never have come to be. Thank you **to everyone mentioned by name in the story** and to everyone not mentioned by name who said A-Okay to the content, for granting me permission to share with the world what I've had the privilege of experiencing with and through you: the Light. And a special shout out to she who opens her home and heart to everyone, Aunt Gu. **To my cousins, siblings, aunts, uncles, grandmother, girlfriends, best good peoples, mentors, and mentees**…for either being completely oblivious to or fully checked-in to this effort and thereby providing the space and grace in which this project could be brought to fruition, for keeping me laughing and wrapped in your care, and for encouraging me to put up shelves. **To my husband Rodell,** for the steadiness of his support, suffering my writerly ways, and being my first full version reader. **To Moses,** who, above and before anyone else, named and believed unequivocally in my calling to be a writer. **To Cruz**, my best good friend, for pushing and yielding in perfect doses, acting as Creative Producer for Endeavor TBD, and for knowing I could do it even when I couldn't. **To Dawan Julien and Will Seamans,** for being advance readers and reviewers, comrades in the struggle, and mighty forces of truth in the world. **To Dia Simms and Nicole Fields** for providing positive feedback and quotes for the back cover. **To Sarah** for being an influential force, acknowledging the dots, and encouraging me to give that Ignite Speech in the first place. **To Naeem,** for providing artist-to-artist encouragements, writing the forward, and inspiring me to keep going even through the pain of the process. **To JaNelle Hanks** for being an author-of-inspiration, who modeled that getting done was possible, and provided practical information on how-to. **To Tracy Stevens of Stray Ink, LLC,** for her graphic design expertise and work on inspirational cover designs and **to Cruz Caldera Creative** for the curve of the dotted path. **To Roser,** for being my family in Barcelona and a fellow traveler on the journey to find peace. And for offering her translator expertise to check all the Spanish and Catalonian words. **To Kathy Murdock,** my trusty content editor, who through equal doses of craft and encouragement was an essential conduit by which this work was made possible. **To Rising Sign Books,** copyeditor and book formatter, who line-by-line made sure this book was ready to go to press. Last but not least, **to Maya,** for saying "so," and through whom I heard the Universe speak.

FOREWORD

By Naeem

Though there were plenty of people around, I was sitting alone on the stairs of the Sacre-Coeur, looking out over the entire city of Paris. It had happened so quickly. One moment I was working on the sandwich line of a Cosi in center city Philadelphia, and the next I was rapping for the indefatigably hip youth of the Parisian underground. And I was a star.

But as I sat looking out over the most beautiful city in the world, I worried about money, management, and record deals.

Then I experienced a moment of clarity and became overwhelmed with a sense of pride. It was my first time in Paris. It was my first time in Europe. I hadn't even had a passport before then. I had always wanted to be a musician on a European tour. And there I was.

I asked myself how a poor little Black boy from Baltimore had gotten himself to the top of a hill, with the Sacre-Coeur's arm around his shoulder, while employing a band of his closest friends. I looked back on the road I had traveled and felt I had forged a path through a jungle by aggressively slashing and burning my way. I had made it through, but it had taken grit to survive.

On Following the Dots presents a different way to find your path, by looking for the route that is marked by serenity, listening for the messages, and discovering a clearer way through.

I was on that hill because the music I had made — in a Brooklyn basement three years before — had brought me to where I had always wanted to be. I was a musician. I was on my dot. If I hadn't taken a walk up to that church alone, I wouldn't have realized I was there.

On Following the Dots posits an alternative way I could have traveled. A way that is about checking in with yourself and not focusing on cutting through resistance, but by following the joy.

Naeem *released the album "Startisha" in June 2020. His music pushes the envelope with roots in Baltimore bass, overtones of retro rock and lyrics full of commentary. Formerly known as Spank Rock, Naeem was a 2019 Pioneer Works Music Resident, and has collaborated with Bon Iver, Santi Gold, Mark Ronson, Boys Noize, and Big Freedia; and has been featured in Interview, the New York Times, Fader Magazine, and Rolling Stone.*

A Note On The Times

In June 2020, as this book is being readied for press, America is in the throes of a civil rights movement — charged forward by the reprehensible deaths of a few, the remembrances of many before them, and the refusal to accept the same fate for the many anticipated to come after...if there is no change. Masses have erupted into the streets demanding the de-militarization of the police, the protection of Black lives, and the de-architecting of systems that inhibit an equitable chance at the pursuit of life, liberty, and happiness. We wonder on the brink of which future we stand: "Are we a nation divided as we fall,"[i] or are we marching toward the truth and justice that will bring us together? Will this be a revolution or will it be war? Maybe both.

At this time, we are also in the middle of a pandemic. The United States has the most COVID19 cases, hospitalizations, and deaths in the world. There were months of stay-at-home orders, but now states are re-opening and record numbers of new cases are being reported. There is disagreement about how to proceed. Some are most worried about health and safety. Others are leading with economics and want to reopen at risk of human cost.

These are unprecedented times, and I wonder if now is right to be talking about dots. Then I realize it is exactly the time. We need to look to where we draw our strength and clarity, figure out how we want to show up in the world, and find the path forward. Now more than ever, we must look for signs from the Universe to tell us who and where we should be.

> *"There is never time in the future in which we will work out our salvation. The challenge is in the moment; the time is always now."*
>
> — James Baldwin

TABLE OF CONTENTS

INTRODUCTION

What Dots Are

J*une 28, 2018* — I'm walking in circles and talking to myself. I've practiced this 5-minute speech repeatedly for a month, but half an hour before show time, I'm outside in a parking lot spazzing out. I drag myself into the beer-tavern-turned-event-hall and hop around the room, weaving in and out of scattered peoplings, making half conversations. My body won't be still. I blitz backstage to run through the talk. Again. I freeze for twenty whole seconds in the middle and rush to ask the speaking coach what to do if that *actually* happens on stage. "There's nothing you can do," he says. "Go with it. Be yourself."

This is not comforting.

My 'self' is the kind of 'self' capable of melting down.

It's the 20th *Ignite Baltimore* and hundreds of people have filled the room waiting for a night of eclectic presentations.

Sixteen speakers get twenty slides and five-minutes each to deliver speeches on topics they believe will spark thought, emotion, and action. A NASA scientist plans to show the latest and greatest pictures of earth from the Hubble Space Telescope. An artist and activist who wants to bring attention to the victims of gun violence through portraiture. A researcher will explain her work imprinting the whiskers of polar bears to track their health and illuminate the environmental changes causing a drastic decline.

I am going to talk about dots.

My natural hair is cut into what I call a Mohawk Mullet. I wear big dangling earrings to demonstrate that it's okay to do so, stand low to the ground at 5'1, and speak with a scratchy voice.

I'm intent on giving air to the multivariate nature of our stories.

Raised in the blue light neighborhoods and street codes of Baltimore City — by matriarchs who would have been academicians had they not been hustlers, and fathers who were difference makers by way of frequent reminder of options — I've graduated from Stanford University, copped an MBA at Johns Hopkins, been a senior leader of organizations, managed millions of dollars, jumped out of a plane, hiked a glacier in Iceland, and zip lined 600ft across a Costa Rican jungle.

I have also been a mess.

A trip-over-my-own-feet, foul-up-big-things, fritzy, dit-zy, who-woulda-thunk-it, all-over-the-place mess.

I've often likened life's journey to one of my favorite movies, the 1986 epic fantasy, *Labyrinth.*[ii] (Fair-warning: there are a few spoilers; just in case you wanna watch it). The heroine inadvertently says magic words and summons a band of goblins. Under cover of night and lightning, they snag her baby brother and whisk him away. He's being held captive in a mystical land by a magic-dancing and stellarly menacing goblin king. He sports stylishly coiffed rock star hair and a shoulder-padded rhinestone ensemble. *Best goblin king ever.*

But anyways….to rescue the kiddo, the protagonist must make her way through a labyrinth. It's a maze of high hedges and briars, gnarly trees, booby traps, and under-ground passageways. There's even a bog of stench — where dipping in one toe leaves someone smelling forever. It's much like, say, the office on a Monday, the record industry during royalty negotiations, America in general, or the dinner table when the conversation has turned toward the upcoming election. It takes skillful navigating to make it out alive, morally intact, and well balanced. The labyrinth is also inhabited by weird creatures. Jim Henson's Muppets have gone wild. Some are troublesome. They can take their heads off and throw them. Some are harmless. Others are helpful. It's hard to tell which. A horned Sasquatch can be quite friendly, but fairies can have a nasty bite. To sort out which creatures are friends or foes, one has to employ the type of emotional intelligence it takes when dealing with, y'know…people.

A maze has been my metaphor for life.

And, for as much as there are ominous woods, there are also unparalleled, magical, soul-feeding experiences, just wanting to be happened upon. The key is getting through the whole winding, unpredictable, messy, and charmed journey by choosing the right roads. Or knowing when to get off the road altogether and find another way.

The key is finding the path…*your* **path.**

Dots are how you find your way through.

I've come to believe there is a path destined for me that I can discover by finding the proverbial lamps that light it: the dots. I believe this is true for all of us.

We can live exemplary, exceptional, ordinary yet extraordinary lives — full of beauty and wonder — as long as we can find our way.

What I'm at Ignite to talk about is *how*. Dots are a guiding concept I've used and spoken of for years. But this is the first time I'm sharing the idea so broadly. I need to get through my anxiety to do so. I take a deep breath, give the queue to start, and begin.[iii]

"Imagine that life is like a connect-the-dots board, and you're moving from place to place, drawing the line, creating the picture that will be your own lived experience. That will be *your* life. But unlike the childhood game, there are infinite dots and no numbers to guide you. Yet, if we want to find our paths, we still have to find our course markers. We still have to find our dots."

I talk about moments when I've been sure I was off or on my path. One was disruptive. I had an anxiety attack, which presented itself as an inability to form words, to get sounds out, and to speak. The other was serene. I knew I was in the right place, having sought to find myself and having actually achieved that.

I share a way to find your dots by asking questions and listening for the Universe's response:

- Where am I?
- Who am I?
- Is this where I'm supposed to be?
- Is this who I'm supposed to be?

I make it to the end of the speech without passing out. I thank everyone for allowing me to be with them standing on one of my dots that day and step down into an audience of smiles and claps. They seem to be happy along with me.

One woman comes up to say thank you with tears coming down her face. She had been having a horrible time at her job and felt hopeless. She told me she was meant to be there to hear the message. Because of it, she knew how she was going to figure out what to do next. We hugged like we'd known each other for a long time, and her response made having pushed through my anxiety worth it. This is the kind of reinforcement the Universe provides — and for which I am always on the lookout.

Here I would like to share the stories that enveloped those two moments. They are drawn from personal writings captured during or very close to the times of the happenings. One is an account of my coming together. One is an account of my falling apart. Both are about finding your way.

I'll also share some perspectives I've gained about navigating the journey, no matter where you are in it.

What I hope you gain is a confirmation of our collective human story, and a way to *find your path* by following the signs and signals that tell you with undeniable clarity you're on it. A way to listen to the Universe by seeing, hearing, feeling, and following the dots.

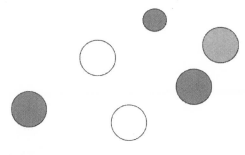

CHAPTER 1

Where I Will Be

J *anuary 4, 2012* — I'm in an open-air plaza with merrymakers of all ages, waiting for a parade. Lights are strung into trees, banjos are being strummed, and costume-wearing toddlers are propped on their fathers' shoulders. I'm surrounded by the dancing syllables of words being exchanged too fast to isolate for understanding. They are conversations spoken and songs sung in a language that is not my native tongue. It's easy to tell by the smiles and laughs and strings of held hands that these are happy times.

No one's paying attention to me. It's lovely.

I've often felt like I had an inscription on my forehead, telling people what ideas they should have about me and how they should or should not engage.

But in this plaza full of people, I feel welcome and invisible. Atypical yet unremarkable. I am like a frog enveloped by a passing school of fish, both observer and participant in the swirl, without any predetermined expectations around how I got to be there or what I should be doing.

I am on a sojourn.
I am there to seek out that which brings joy.

I had arrived in Spain with a return ticket for two months later and a little hesitation around being a woman traveling and living alone in a place so far away.

But I'd already gone from the red-bricked rowhomes, down-southish backyard fish fries, and chaotic familiarity of West Baltimore, to the all-day-all-night people-filled streets, glamor-and-grunge, and if-you-can-make-it-here-you-can-make-it-anywhere appeal of Manhattan, with favorable results.

A couple years after finishing undergrad, I returned to my hometown of Baltimore for the professional opportunities, close friends, and tight-knit family there. I had the phenomenal chance to be a staffer at one of the nation's foremost non-profits in responsible fatherhood and workforce development. I had advanced from entry level to senior management — helping to incubate programs, secure funding, and provide training and technical assistance to organizations across the nation.

Annnd — even though I had vowed not to — I had gotten caught up in the frenzy, hype, and drama that can come with being from and *of* the hood. In early 2008, I had just resolved a court case that had ensued from a roommate disagreement; and I desperately needed to end a relationship that had all the plotlines of a soap opera. We celebrated Valentine's on National Side Chick's Day, and despite their sardonic and quite hysterical underpinnings, my jokes rarely elicited from him any laughs.

So, empowered by a sister who would keep my house safe, a best friend who offered a shared mattress on the floor of a Brooklyn sublet, and a newly minted graduate business degree that provided professional cover, I ran to New York — seeking distance's aid in getting away from some things and over others.

In New York, I worked as a senior manager for a health and human services non-profit that provided residential housing to people with developmental disabilities and high school completion options for young people who were over-aged and under-credited.

And most importantly, I grew all the way up. Though I was twenty-nine when I arrived and thirty-four when I left, I'll always credit my time in the city with when I actually became a functioning adult.

I made some of my best girlfriends. They taught me how to tie a ribbon straight. They created a safe and vulnerable space for me to learn to cry properly, like a boss. Without shame or explanation, as a right, and a route forward. I exercised choices in ways I had previously found inaccessible and created my own new norms. My girlfriends and I would meet for brunch wearing whatever we wished — a sequined dress or skinny jeans with a stretched-out tank top — based on how we were feeling that day and our own brands of unique flair.

I disrupted unhealthy understandings and replaced them with healthier ones. I had a relationship that completely reset my idea of what courtship, kindness, and mutual admiration looked like. Closed heart places were opened under the care of a younger, gentler spirit who showed me how to hold hands.

I became a resident tourist. Learned to soak up, eat up, and enjoy. I saw the Lion King on Broadway. Ate papaya salad and spicy noodles at a chef's table. Turned shots upside-down into frozen margaritas at Dallas BBQ's.

I discovered firsthand what I'd only heard about in books and took away poignant impressions and realizations. I visited Ellis Island. Heard the stories of immigrants in first person account. And came to deeply understand that it is decidedly not the story of how my people got here.

I went to the historic Coney Island and rode the rides I'd seen in archival film. I huffed and puffed, walking up to the crown of the Statue of Liberty. The ranger was elated to see people, as not many choose to keep climbing after the elevators stop.

I'd lived where the essence of greatness had lived. I found a studio apartment on the historic Strivers Row, where the literary zeniths of the Harlem Renaissance — James Baldwin, Maya Angelou, and Zora Neale Hurston — witnessed, recorded, and reported their experience of being *other* in America.

New York was pivotal, but I knew from the day I arrived that I would eventually leave. It was a place I had gone to grow, but not to stay.

After a few years, the day-to-day started to wear. I tired of the fourth floor walkup to my apartment. I no longer wanted to carry what seemed like fifty pounds of laundry — in a military-style rucksack slung over my shoulder — down those fifty-three steps, across three city blocks to the laundry mat, and back. And when I'd take the bus down to Maryland for a visit, I found myself saying, "Hi trees. There you are. I miss you."

I felt it was coming — the time to move on to whatever was next. But I didn't know what next was. As a part of figuring that out, I decided to step out on a limb and do something unorthodox. I took a gap-year (right when I was moving from early to mid-career, when lots of people might say you can't, but you absolutely can).[iv]

I resigned from my job and utilized my life's savings to cover expenses while working on projects that I wouldn't have been able to otherwise. I worked as an independent consultant and helped musician, Spank Rock, launch his first independent album, including getting to go on tour with the band. I also made space to exercise my body and clear my mind.

Months in, the gap was working. With a cleared field of vision and expanded bandwidth to tackle the "what's next" question, an answer surfaced. I started to fervently desire settling my grown-up self in to *home*.

But there was a smallish problem. As grown up as I knew I was, I hadn't quite confirmed who exactly I had grown up to be. And as much as I longed for home, I didn't know where exactly that was anymore.

I had utilized my savings well and still had a few more months of living expenses in the stash. That gave me a little time to figure out where I was going to land. I asked myself if it was necessary to stay in New York while I was sorting that out.

That question led to phone calls and emails to friends all over to see if they knew where I could be. I asked about condos on the beach in the Florida Keys, cabins in the quiet parts of the Midwest, or even accommodations in other countries, as I'd always wanted to live abroad.

A friend of a friend knew someone who could be any-where in the world doing his work and introduced us. Through emails and phone calls, we went from strangers connected by one person, to two people on opposite sides of the Atlantic Ocean ready to do each other a relatively uncommon, mutually beneficial favor. We would swap our apartments; he would live in my apartment in Harlem, New York, NY, and I would head to his place in Barcelona, Catalonia, Spain. I would go on a sojourn, in search of myself and *home*.

ON FOLLOWING THE DOTS

I don't know it yet, but I am looking for the dots.

I am looking for signs so clear that they confirm my path.

In the plaza, a parade starts and the Three Kings traipse around the crowd, legs high and scepters raised. Families clap along to traditional songs. Fuzzy angel wings, halos, and scarves bounce to the beat, catching gently on the crisp nighttime air. I am dumfounded with wonder, not sure how it came to pass that without any planning or prior knowledge, I had arrived in Spain on the day before Three Kings Day. On this special night, children leave their shoes out, hoping that when they wake up in the morning, the three wise men will have left gifts inside or beside them. I am a bright-eyed wanderer who dropped in, not knowing what I'd find. And I had arrived on something like Christmas Eve.

Go

> *"She's got her ticket. I think she's going to use it. I think she's going to fly away."*
> Tracy Chapman

Navigating through the maze of life takes having the courage to *go*. Courage is needed to discover what awaits on the other side of fear.

Courage is pushing through stage fright to deliver a message that a stranger desperately needed to hear.

It is walking out of a plane's open hanger into the clouds to see a patchwork quilt of green and yellow earth viewable only from inside the whirling sky.

Courage is dumping dudeo and risking the looming possibility of ending up alone, but instead finding a relationship where there was actually a lot of time spent laughing at each other's jokes.

No matter where you are in the journey — on or off your path — you'll need the courage to do things that scare you.

I first left Baltimore when I was eighteen, flying ~2,500 miles across the country to start college, sight unseen. I hadn't even been to California before. I remember traveling on the airplane, brimming with anticipation and optimism. I sat between a father who had read books with me since I was born[v] and a stepfather who had inspired me to aspire higher.

The trip to drop me off at one of the most prestigious universities in the nation was the fruit of their labor and the labor of many. College was ripe with the opportunity to make my idyllic adolescent dreams come true and to make the rag-tag, rabble-rousing Baltimore kindred from which I hailed proud. People would later remark at how brave I was to have gone, but I hadn't been.

When I arrived on campus, I was admittedly, unpleasantly insecure. I got stunted at a registration table, unsure about how to approach the alphabetic placard that corresponded to the first letter of my last name. But, there was no doubt I would be fine. Starting college felt exciting, prescribed, and safe.

At thirty-three, however, even as a self-professed adult, when I was headed to Barcelona and wanted to make it on my own, I was *absolutely unsure* if I could. It was the first time I had done something I truly considered brave. Flying to another country, alone, having to figure *it* out, without knowing what *it* was exactly. There wouldn't be any placards telling me where to stand.

The worst-case scenario was that I would get there, not be able to function, and have to abbreviate the trip and come back. The best case was that the trip would be positively life affirming. The courageous thing had been going and giving myself no option but to find out which.

A courageous act played out in the movies often looks like someone charging head-on into battle while a triumphant soundtrack plays. For instance, when the labyrinth-traversing heroine and her band of misfit friends arrive at the outer gates of the castle, the metal giant who guards the door is swinging an oversized axe to keep them out. Someone rushes to the rescue, hurling himself off a wall and on top of the giant to disable it.

But, eh, courage isn't like that in real-life. At least, not for me. It is inhaling gulps of air, watching my hands shake, hearing my voice quiver, and speaking up

> *"My fear is my only courage."*
> Bob Marley

anyway. As someone who can be overwhelmed by anxiety around what *could* happen, and who can be scared about anything — and sometimes just about everything — if I stopped every time I was afraid, I would barely do anything at all. I have a long-standing deal with myself: it's okay to be afraid, but go anyway.

If you can sense that fear is standing in the way of something good — an accomplishment, a repair, an essential next step — don't wait for the fear to clear. It may not. Move forward as soon as you can. Go.

Even if you're uncomfortable, *especially* if you're uncomfortable. That's what happened when I booked that ticket to Spain. I wasn't sure I was ready, but I went.

If you can muster the courage to move toward your intentions, you'll find taking fearful leaps is what gets you most of the way there.

**So… Go. Your next dot is often on
the other side of fear.**

CHAPTER 2

Where I Am

October 20, 2016 — Four years after I'd stood in a plaza, full of awe — on the eve of the first full day of an adventure — I am unsteady, full of dread, and on the verge of losing it.

It's after ten pm and I'm on the phone frantically talking to my little sister. My thoughts aren't linear. There's no filter. Some sentences I'm finishing. Some I'm not. I'm tripping over words. I'm asking for help.

My cell phone headset is plugged in and both hands are on the steering wheel of my Volkswagen Beetle. I'm meandering through side streets. I'm half trying to find the way back to my friend's house where I'm staying for the night. I'm half circling through the upper alphabet blocks of the nation's capital, going nowhere.

This is not a dot. Something's not right. I am figuratively and literally lost.

I am having a breakdown.

My sister Maya and I grew up in different households. And our six-year age difference mattered when we were small. Most of our lives we'd been fond but not too familiar. We'd only gotten to know each other closely when I moved to New York and she had come to be steward of the west Baltimore row home I had left behind for a spell. And when I returned several years later and moved back into the house with her and my brother, she and I would become the fastest and deepest of friends. We'd later move into a duplex on the eastside that we found and rehabbed together. She and her husband lived downstairs in one unit. My husband and I lived upstairs in the other. We had each other's keys and alarm codes. She often broke in to steal a pot when she didn't have one big enough to prepare lentils or quinoa with coconut milk or whatever pesci-vegan dish pretty brown girls who go to the gym for a living eat. And apart from her considering most utility items in my place borrowable without notice, she is my salvation. We sort out how to not suck at life by sharing perspectives from kindred vantage points. We afford each other latitude, but no escape from hearing the sometimes warm, sometimes not-too-warm, blunt truth delivered from someone who cares. Sometimes, all I need is my sister.

I was 38, and she was 32 at the time of the frantic conversation while driving in circles. I was the operations executive in charge of finance, information technology, data, compliance, office management, and human resources for a successful non-profit youth development and community engagement organization. The organization has two dozen staff, a multi-million-dollar budget, and multiple locations around Baltimore City.

A couple hours earlier, I had missed an important finance meeting. I had missed the call — totally failed to dial-in, totally failed to let anyone know — because I simply and wholly forgot. For. Got. Completely. And not so conveniently, had plugged my phone in to charge in another room. That meant I had also missed texts from a colleague asking where I was and if I was okay.

To me, missing the call was a biggish deal. I was the-lead-finance-person-at-the-organization and failed to attend a finance meeting I had set the agenda for and was supposed to run. Yeah…*run*. It was *my* meeting, y'know…the one I forget.

When I had first landed this executive job, I had said I was sure I was on my dot. Before then, I had been back from New York and living in Baltimore again, but was working forty miles south in Washington DC, at a community-centered design firm that supported national and international initiatives. The firm was all about fueling movements by entrepreneurs and intrepreneurs. And though I enjoyed the work, had many one-of-a-kind colleagues who became close friends, and had become through osmosis a practicing design thinker, I had become quite tired of the daily travel.

For two-and-a-half years, I had spent three hours a day going back and forth on the commuter train. I have heard lore of a study that says happiness in life is inversely correlated to the length of one's commute. And I can attest to that firsthand. Long, daily train rides are bad, just bad. When I came back from New York, I had reached out to a bunch of people to let them know I was back in town and wanted to connect, but I had barely seen anyone. I was leaving the house at 6AM and returning at 7:30PM, too tired to go anywhere. Finding a role near where I lived meant I could regain three hours of my day and eliminate the risk of dying of acute-commute-related-exhaustion or I-keep-missing-out-on-happy-hour-distress. So, when I got the job at the Baltimore-based youth development organization close to home — a fifteen-minute walk, in fact — I gladly took the 20% pay cut.

And, I was excited to contribute to a mission that served the city I love.

See, Baltimore bore me, and I am madly, truly, and deeply in love. Real love. The kind of love that allows you to see promise in all dimensions, aspects, and nuances in the object of your affection. The kind of love that allows you to look past the afflictions and see through to the soul, feeling that you, yourself, are part of that soul; a giver and receiver, an amplifier of the other-worldly spirit. I love Baltimore as if I bore it. The kind of love where you feel blessed to have been part of a special moment even if that moment carried with it immense pain. I see the acute endemic and systemic issues battering us, and watch the news stories about the number of people we lose to violence and think not, "We are hopeless" but instead, "We can do better."[vi] We can recognize the magnitude of our own beauty, the latitude of our reach, the intensity of our power, and the depth of our abilities — diligence, artistry, intellect, fight, indomitable will — embattled by our collective struggle. When we realize our greatness, our Light will shine bright enough for all the heavens and earth to see. That kind of love.

And, I felt like I had happened upon a chance to come *all the way home* in a way much deeper than geographically. The organization encouraged giving people the latitude to be themselves and to connect with each other regardless of perceived differences and in that way create community. If they had actually figured that out, then maybe I could also. Maybe I could bring my full self to the fore and be welcome. Parts of me, no matter how true, were still being disallowed.

See, my 'self' has often been forced to break down into pieces. To never quite make visible the sum total of who I am. I cannot be a late 1800s / early 1900s art buff *and* think Tupac is a prophet.[vii] I cannot develop multi-tabbed financial spreadsheets *and* drop out the innards of words and phrases. Because Picasso's blue period can be as alien on a porch on Poplar Grove[viii] as "i'on'tno" can be concerning in the Board Room. So, I have tended to hide a little or a lot, to assimilate a tad or massively, to co-opt or code; to avoid exposing the delicate and incompressible intricacies that make me an individual human being, like everyone else. Or risk confusing or scaring people by being too much of something they don't understand or too little of something they thought I would be. I have often felt compelled to contort myself in such a way that the sides that show are the ones that make those around me most comfortable. Through this learned assimilation, I've come to be fluent in the dialects and decorum of many circumstances, many rooms, and many walks. I well-traverse seemingly disparate worlds and feel that parts and pieces of me belong almost everywhere and with almost everyone. But, I am rarely showing up whole. At sparse times, I feel safe to drift fully into the unfiltered version of myself; to say or do whatever comes to mind; to be at play and at peace. But in many moments, I am not free.

But, after I had been on my dot and thought I would have finally been able to come 'all the way home' and 'bring myself altogether,' *I am falling apart.*

I am in **a hole.**

I am driving around aimlessly, rambling to my sister. I batter through the story about missing the board call. I try to get her to understand why it's alarming. I explain the physical sensations in my body — tingling like when you touch your tongue to a battery.

Thoughts speed in and out of my head. "I am a fraud." "I can't handle this." "I signed up for this." "I let things get out of hand until they spin out of control." I make her listen to the happenings of the previous months that had provided pushes toward disruption. I try to explain how this *one* missed phone call — for which I immediately apologized and got a cordial, "no worries" type of response — happened to be *the thing* that opened me up to hearing the Universe saying, "You are in trouble. You are in lot of trouble. Do something. Now."

I say to my sister, "I need a break. Right now. I need a break."

I tell her I want to ask for emergency and immediate time off from my job. Then I ask her a fear-filled, permission-seeking, all-in question, "Are they going to think I'm crazy?"

"Maybe," she says. "But does it matter?" She's not being flip. The question is warmly and authentically asked.

I tell her my fear that even asking for a break will send up an alarm that I might not be able to un-ring. A potentially career-ending alarm that takes away options for my future.

She says, "**So.** You have to do what you have to do."

This is why I'm talking to my sister. She'on't care 'bout nuffin' but the things that matter. She says words out her mouf. Words right in the center, not in the margins. Words you can't avoid.

When she says, "So," she means, "If you're breaking down, then you are breaking down. And if they see it, then they see it. You have to do what you have to do to take care of yourself."

I breathe in deeply. Let her advice fall over me. I calm down. Feeling relieved. Feeling defeated. Feeling relieved that at least I know I feel defeated.

"Buuuuuut, I don't wanna," I whine.

This is a break-through whine. This is me with clarity, being sad, being scared, letting myself feel whatever I am feeling, and making peace.

The rest of the call is comforting. She tells me it's okay. I say I'm grateful for her. We hang up.

I find the way back to my friend's house where I shelter for the night. And real early the next morning, I text my boss, saying, "We need to talk." She doesn't ask any questions and says to come over to her satellite office. On the hour drive up I-95, I think of what I am going to say.

I walk into her office and launch right in. "This is going terribly wrong."

At the time of that conversation, I believe most people in my professional microcosm would have characterized me as well liked and successful. My family would have said I was the shiggidity shid shid or doin' big things, or something like that. Since graduating from college and entering the workforce, I had been relatively professionally accomplished, having roles that had increased in responsibility, pay, and breadth. I'm known for having a vocal irreverence for the status quo; have been told I am uncommonly tenacious; and when I am not on a tear about results, some would say I'm kinda fun. Sometimes I sing my words or often break into spontaneous bad dance, like my mother did; compute with sticky notes; and have a deep interest in getting things done well (and on budget) while incorporating some laughs along the way. Apart from scattered occurrences of muck ups — small and grand but separated far enough from each other, like uneaten green peas a kid has spread out on the plate — I had built a solid professional record and enjoyed an expanding network of amazing people, who had become my mentors, advocates, colleagues, and friends.

And in this particular operations exec role, I had lead a team of staff and contractors through building and launching a technology app. I was working with well-regarded corporations and non-profit organizations to start an innovative collaboration, which included constructing new office space. My team was handling a myriad of day-to-day items, ranging from installing Wi-Fi to hiring new staff. And on top of all that, I had assumed a prominent role in actualizing the organization's vision of bringing people together.

But there was something going awry: the audit. For those who haven't been through one, in a financial audit, independent accountants access the organization's financial records. They check to see if the accounting has been done correctly and deliver a report. An audit happens yearly and a good report lets donors and stakeholders know the organization is financially sound, which is important, of course.

As the finance lead, I was responsible for overseeing the audit and making sure it went well. The problem was, in previous jobs, I had worked with accountants. But this team was structured differently, and I had to figure out how to get the audit done without one. My two-person finance crew was learning as we went, but as the auditing firm's questions got harder, the figuring-out-as-we-went meant there were delays in preparing the materials for review.

And months into the process, old but persistent personal habits of mine had surfaced, and made a tough situation near professionally catastrophic. I was flat-out avoiding the auditors. I had stopped responding to their emails, stopped taking their phone calls, and stopped listening to their voicemails.

And though having to address this awry audit and face a personal vice of procrastination — which I had not been able to best for the entirety of my adolescent or adult life — would have been quite enuf to unsteady the proverbial ground on which I stood and send me careening into an acute crisis…that was, not nearly, all of it.

There was, eh…the rest of the job and all the other worky stuff that comes with trying to do things that are hard. The pressure that comes along with being viewed as, the shiggidity shid shid. Trying to sort out what it meant to integrate my 'self.' My full, active, regular, y'know, real-life — complete with goals and responsibilities that have little to do with the aforementioned. Family and friends with whom I wanted to spend time and be in community. Loved ones in need and/or in struggle. The earth. The news. My physical health. And an underlying and consistent consciousness toward the refinement of my soul, so that when it comes time for me to try to pass through to the next plane, I make it.

Annnd…if you haven't noticed yet…I'm Black, y'all. I'm Blackety Black, Black Black, y'all[ix] in a world that is dangerously inhospitable for my people.

And, if I cannot escape the context of our society and the realities of everyday existence levied on me for having been born into a particular time, into a particular body, and as a member of a particular caste, then neither can my stories.

I was a mess, in a mess. Trapped in a place of doubt and fear. Giving more than I had. And feeling like that wasn't good enough.

The ground had given way beneath my feet. I was aggressively slipping down. Gravity was stuffing me into a vertical canal of me-sized diameter: a hole.

The missed meeting was what woke me up to the reality that I was falling. I had finally heard the Universe's small, still voice.

Something was going terribly wrong.

Watch Out for Holes

> *"Not everything that is faced can be changed, but nothing can be changed until it is faced."*
>
> James Baldwin

A hole in the road is a crisis you have to deal with because it's all-encompassing. It has swallowed you.

Holes are tricky, dark places that you can fall into due to a myriad of things — disappointment about a college graduation cancelled during the pandemic; the first time you've felt terror, having become fully sentient to real threats of bodily harm because of the skin you wear; guilt caused by backsliding into behaviors you thought you'd overcome. Holes can swallow you due to circumstances out of your control, something you had a hand in, or some part of both.

If you're in a hole, you can't see your dots. You've got to climb out to get back on the path.

When I was in high school, I would show up on test day not having studied at all, participate in a quick lunchtime run through of key terms, and get an A on the afternoon's exam. Throughout the entirety of my academic career and late into my professional one, excellence in some areas made up

> *"Be kinder than is necessary, for everyone you meet is fighting some kind of battle."*
>
> J. M. Barrie

for a penchant toward procrastination in others. Sometimes, I'd rally late in the game and earn a win. Sometimes not. And frequently enough, I'd make plan after plan and then not do anything at all. Delay turned into avoidance, avoidance turned into neglect, and neglect resulted in disrepair. I have A's and F's on my undergraduate transcript; I have been on both academic excellence and academic suspension lists.

Over time, as the things I was responsible for became more consequential and the routes to the finish lines more complex, late in the game rallies became less effective. And though my tendency to procrastinate had waned — reeled in by systems I developed to manage myself and my projects — it remained an underlying part of how I might show up.

And still, things had generally continued to work out…until they hadn't.

I'd reached the point where that habit needed to end or the impacts would be steep. But I didn't come to this understanding through foresight. I came to it by a crash.

That's what holes are like. You find yourself in a disastrous situation, a dark place, unable to trace back the steps that got you there. You just know it can't work out well if you stay where you are.

So…watch out for holes, the ones we dig for ourselves, the ones the world makes for us, and everything in between.

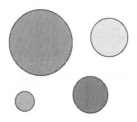

CHAPTER 3

A Sojourn in Barcelona

March 6, 2012 - I am on a flight back from Spain. I had spent two months unencumbered — seeing, touching, tasting, hearing, and being a part of things. And by doing so, I figured out what I liked to see, touch, taste, hear, and be a part of. I had mapped my own route through the maze and had met with rigor the happy little secrets I had known would be waiting along the way, but whose form I couldn't have predicted. I had walked slowly through those moments and found a defined self within them. And I was bringing that 'self' back home to where I had discovered home to be.

Every day, I had followed the joy.

This is the account.

January 4, 2012 — I am a part of wherever here is. It took an eight-hour plane ride, then three hours to get through immigration, out of baggage claim, off an airport shuttle to the metro train, and from the metro stop to a cobblestone side street called Carrer San Pere I Miguel. There stood a salmon-colored four-storied building.

An English-speaking woman lets me in to the apartment and we go up to the third floor. She teaches me how to use the keys, and then I watch her disappear quickly down the stairs. I stand in disbelief. I made it.

I go into the apartment, put my bags down by the door, and look around. The place is railroad-style, with a living room with two bright red chairs and a window that looks out over a garage and a pub on the corner. I can see people passing by on the street. There are two bedrooms, an office, and a little patio off the kitchen that houses the washing machine and access to a clothesline out the back window to dry. The bathroom shower has dark blue tile that appears hand-blotted and glazed. Instead of an overhead shower, there's a handheld sprayer. The walls are decorated with references to cinema and media, framed classic movie posters — like Jekyll and Hyde and Charlie's Angels — and iconic magazine and record covers. There are lots of books; a bookshelf in the living room has hundreds, and a side table in the hallway has a few rare ones on display. Empty bottles with detailed, colorful labels serve as bookends. Everything is meant to be both pretty and functional.

There's an orchid and a few potted cacti. It's a cozy and well-kept place.

It looks like the person who lives there loves it.

I go out. It's winter, but not too cold outside. I'm wearing my tweed jacket and a fuchsia scarf and blend in with locals wearing smallish coats to take off the nip. I'm staying in a neighborhood called Horta, in the northern part of Barcelona. It's a bit of a ways out from the more notable and metropolitan, touristy areas of the city. It feels like a municipality of its own and people call it a town.

I walk around exploring. There are shopping strips with utility stores that sell pharmaceuticals, electronics, and clothing. There are several small grocery stores. There is a large, open-air market where one can get fresh just-about-anything — fish, beef, chicken, fruit, all kinds of cheese, and a myriad of vegetables — some of which I've never seen, and most of which I have no skill to prepare.

There are locally owned shops and restaurants, quaint bars, and coffee shops. Sometimes a few are lined up together on a busy-esque thoroughfare, and sometimes one is tucked in, hidden out of the way.

On side streets, there are multi-colored houses with flowering vines crawling up stucco façades, looking as if they've been fabricated for made-for-TV- movies.

As I get a lay of the land, there appear to be mini neighborhoods within the larger one, each with its own individual character and pattern of people traffic. Not too far from the apartment, there is a public square with tables and chairs. It is early afternoon and hundreds of people are suddenly starting to spill into it, walking through to get from one place to the other, picking a table and having lunch with friends, or busying themselves running errands in and out of the shops that line the perimeter. I understand it to be siesta, which is not a nap but a real couple-hours' break in the middle of the day.

I'd taken entry-level Spanish courses in college, and in preparation for the trip, I had brushed up with a tutor. Before I'd left the States, I had convinced myself I knew just enough Spanish.

I did not.

I go into a shop. I try to explain to the patron what type and shape of electrical adaptor I need to charge my phone. He doesn't understand me and tries to say what I might mean before shaking his head and shooing me off. It takes me no less than an hour and a half and visits to six different shops, distressing patrons with my inadequate dialect, but I pick up words and phrases with every interaction, and eventually I get the adaptor.

I go back to the apartment, charge my electronics, and check-in with my family and friends to let them know I'm more than okay. Then I rest a bit before I plan to go back outside that evening. I hear there is going to be some kind of parade.

January 7, 2012 — *I recognize change.* Locals are very proud to be from Horta, and I am proud to adopt myself as a local. For the first few days I'd gone wherever I could go, exploring beyond my neighborhood, to the whole city to get a good sense of where I was and what was out there.

There were enough differences that made me feel like a foreigner. The subway was extraordinarily clean and fast, and I never waited more than five minutes for a train; it was nothing like in New York with the congestion on the platform, intermittent bathroom smells, and sometimes dueling patrons who made for a typically interesting subway travel experience. I also learned that in many places, Spanish — which I had inadequately practiced — is the second language. The first and preferred language is Catalan, to which I was wholly unfamiliar.

But there were many familiarities. My neighborhood was just the suburbs. Regular people were living their daily lives, wearing slacks and heading to work. And then there was me, decidedly not wearing slacks, decidedly not heading to work, learning to be where I was without any of that.

I am in a small, yellow-lit coffee shop with a few tables and a kind patron who makes conversation with customers who sit and drink their morning coffees, rather than taking them to go. In front of me is a book I have been working on for ten years. It is a work of fiction set in the 1990s Baltimore of my teenaged years. It chronicles the untoward befalling's and running's amuck in the life of a terse, funny, and esoteric protagonist who has a knack for achievement and a habit of being a tad bit reckless.

I'd always keenly identified with the main character — a hyperbolic personification of what it is like to be both victim and instigator of the fray. But it had been a long time since I'd sat with her to come up with her thoughts, actions, and motivations. As I sit, not only does the character feel distant, but so does the author. The book feels written by someone I no longer am. I have far fewer thorns than when I first wrote it.

January 8, 2012 — I seek family. When I first met Roser, she talked fast and smiley; had an anything is possible attitude; wore dark, curly hair falling vivaciously down onto her shoulders in agreement with her personality; and was in Harlem plump and pregnant with her first child, far away from family and friends in her hometown in Spain. She had come to Manhattan with her husband, who was on a business rotation at work. I remember being amazed that she was traveling at all. I had thought pregnant women didn't do that. They weren't out and about in unfamiliar places; they were supposed to be nesting or something like that. And there she was, gallivanting around a metropolitan city as springily as her belly would allow, adventuring. It was like she hadn't even heard of any such constraints around what she was *supposed* to be doing. Just by meeting her, I felt let into a fantastic secret.

We get to decide where we go, what we do, and what we think. The possibilities in our lives are more open than they seem.

Since we'd met, she had moved back to Barcelona. She is the one who introduced me to David, the apartment swapper, and how I knew even before I met him that he was good people.

Roser is my safe haven. Knowing her makes me feel like I have a place in case something goes wrong. A friend. A family.

I go to meet up with her (+1 on the way), her husband and their two-and-half-year-old in Eixample Esquerre. It literally means left extension, and the neighborhood is on the left side of Passeig de Gràcia, a huge center-city paved walk with hundreds of stores ranging from high-end Louis Vuitton and Yves St. Laurent to mom-and-pop shops that sell household wares for around a dollar. There were a myriad of restaurants and eateries and some museums too. It's like Rodeo Drive meets Times Square with more ornate architecture and pedestrians who walk with a chiller gait.

We sit at a table to have café con leche. Her daughter sits across from me, barely tall enough to see over the edge of the table. She's a mini of her mother with bouncy dark brown locks — lively, smart, and gregarious. She speaks Catalan and Spanish and is patient when she tries to engage me in conversation.

Roser gives me tips on how to navigate the city, and tells me of the places I should make sure I go before I'm done, like Tibidabo, a castle up on a hill, and Ribes de Fresser, a town in the mountains of Catalonia where many go to ski. It can be reached by a long train ride. Her family used to take hikes in the hills there when she was a child.

I log it all as best as I can but take the most care in remembering where she lives, how to get there by metro, and how to call them if I need. We give kisses and hugs, and I strike off, knowing I will see them sparingly. I am to only call or run to them if necessary.

January 11, 2012 — *I am worldly.* By chance, friends Lihua and Boresch are visiting from New York. Lihua is a Chinese woman who's quite a bit prettier than most of us have ever enjoyed. She has a fluttering, birdlike spirit, but walks demurely on the ground. Boresch is her boyfriend, a real estate broker who talks expressively with his hands. They traveled to Barcelona from Brooklyn to visit his childhood friend, Emiliano. We went out to explore the edgy, artsy neighborhoods, eat tapas in El Born, visit Galeria H20 in Gràcia, and drink beer in a rooftop garden overlooking gently lit streets. We saw a photography exhibit about transplant patients and a top-secret lamp prototype created by the architect gallery owner.

At Emiliano's parents' house, his dad makes a traditional Catalonian mushroom and beef dish. We spoon the deliciousness into our mouths and drink glass upon glass of red wine, heavy in alcohol content. The table conversation takes place in five principal languages — Catalan, Spanish, French, English, and Esperanto, an almost extinct tongue that Emiliano's dad studies and speaks as a hobby. Boresch and Emiliano get up to play some songs on the piano and guitar, and we listen intently and sway. "Good nights," exchange from all over the globe, including in Chinese and something close to German, but not quite. It is like being granted entrance into an underground collective of multi-lingual socialites, who are cool without trying, right out of a scene in an indie film.

January 12, 2012 — I am lulled by the blues. A few state-side friends, who know people living in the area, have said I should meet up with their connections. So far, I know Roser, in case of emergencies and Emiliano, for hanging out. I'm on my way to meet my Denver-based friend's Irish cousin, who works as a costume designer for the movies, and her beau, Kenny, a teacher and musician. We meet at El Bistro, a bar that's about twelve feet across and likely only twice as deep. The walls are wood paneling and tables are jammed in.

Everyone seems to know each other.

A three-person band is performing blues songs in English. Two guitar players are perched on backless stools, and one slim guy is belting soothing and aerated vocals full of more promise than melancholy. After a few songs, Kenny jumps in with the harmonica. His cheeks expand quickly in and out. He taps his leg, controlling the quiver of the fingers that enwrap the tiny instrument. It emits a room full of sound; it's as if the violin and trumpet have a lovechild that sings a dancy blues.

After the show, he introduces me to the lead singer, a friend and fellow musician, Nathan. He's an Englishman who's been in Barcelona for years, teaching, singing, and painting. He speaks with a softened British accent or in perfect Spanish with rounded vowel sounds and prudent consonants. He has pulling blue eyes and an infectious spirit. He offers to walk me to the metro when the evening's over. I say yes and give the cousins kisses goodnight.

We are in Barceloneta, the part of the city farthest south, right along the Mediterranean Sea. The people here live in flats with balconies that overlook the sand. He says, "It is near criminal to be so close to the ocean and not go." So, we take a detour and walk a couple of blocks. It's not long before there's the crush of sand on the bottom of our shoes and we can hear the gentle roar of a quiet sea. Behind us lights glow off in the distance and out in front of us there's blue water painted black by the night — a void of possibilities somewhere over the brink. It is like staring off the edge of a page.

We feel the brisk air whistle in and watch waves break against the shore. I sit on his jacket, tuned into the sound of his voice. We talk about how we'd come to be there, right then.

January 19, 2012 — I am inspired by art. I had already spent a particularly gorgeous day walking through Parc de la Ciutadella and had shared overexposed photos cast with an illuminating glow because the technically correct photos had failed to show how enchanting the place truly was. I imagined Alice fell down her rabbit hole in some place similar.

I'd gone to an exhibit in the Caixa Forum, and Impressionists, Monet, Renoir, and Degas were present — they are my favorites and I go see them whenever their canvases travel to a museum nearby. At the forum, their work is abundant and as lovely as ever. Up close, the works are indiscernible strokes, spots, and smatterings of paint. And upon stepping back, the splatters merge and depict vivid landscapes and vibrant scenes of humans acting and interacting. They transmit a range of sentiment that impress upon the humans viewing the aura of the things themselves.

French tourists had called me "cousin, cousin" to get my attention so I would snap a photo of them and when I responded in Spanish, they seem confused. I didn't speak the language they thought we shared.

I walk through the Picasso Museum and read every single placard. I have a notepad and record details from the ones that strike me. I paraphrase that in 1900, Picasso went off to Paris and discovered impressionists Cezanne, Lautrec,

Bonnard, and Van Gogh; and first started producing colorful works largely inspired by these artists. Then, from 1901 to 1904, he fell into his well-known blue period. In 1917, he followed a ballerina back to Barcelona and launched into cubism.[x]

I am inspired that he was inspired by the impressionists just as I am. I think back to my own one-color period in college, where I painted only in brown because I felt there wasn't enough brown around. And I am soothed by the thought that it must be just about everyone who is drawn in by ballerinas and by Barcelona.

I think of all the times I've wanted to go through a museum at my own pace, but had felt rushed by someone or something outside of myself — a museum companion who thinks that art is interesting but not *that* interesting, or an engagement I had planned afterward and needed to hurry to make.

Yet here I am, seeing every work, only the art and what it sparks within me dictating the cadence of my stride. I don't have anywhere I'd rather be.

January 21, 2012 — I believe in the law of attraction. After leaving the beach, Nathan said, "I would like to see you again."

And here we are, seeing each other again. He invites me up to see his paintings, circles and swirls of vivid color that wrap around each other fluidly. He tells me how he would like to have a girlfriend. I am quiet mostly except for smiles in his direction, trying not to look overrun with girly giddiness. Though I am. He says we should have dinner. He walks me to the train and kisses me on the cheek.

As the train careens toward Horta, I am smiling. How I love these things — to hear, "I would like to see you again," and to be invited "up" — and to know that someone I like, likes me too.

I marvel at how elusive such things have been in the past. But now, with how much sweet ease they seem to float from him to me and stick like dust on my skin, as soon as I had let what was on the inside seep out.

January 22, 2012 — *I get along with the even thoughs.* In the grocery stores and markets, there's not much quick food to pour in a pot and heat. And in the apartment, there's no microwave, so even though I've never had cause to do so before, I'll have to learn how to cook. I visit the world-famous Boqueria mega, open-air market. The stands in the front have tourist prices, so I shop in the back and buy avocados and fresh chicken for less than half the price.

When I get back to the kitchen, I can't bake the poultry. I don't know how to work the oven. I knock on Magdalena's (the neighbor's) door. She comes over, looks at the appliance, says immediately that all ovens are different, she doesn't know this particular one, lighting it could be dangerous, and that I should call David's mother to show me how, so I don't cause a fire.

She stays and tells me stories from her childhood and even though I understand very little of the words, it's enough to get a sense of what it was like for her growing up. She also gives me instructions on preparing chicken wings on the stovetop with white wine, a little salt, garlic, and olive oil.

Even though I can't use the oven, I know how to light the stovetop burner. I turn on the gas and use a metal clicker to create a spark that ignites the flame. The flame whooshes out before it calms, and then I turn the dial and lower the flame to one that's calm and usable.

January 24, 2012 — *I look to grow in my awareness.* For a long time, if anyone asked me for adjectives to describe myself, I would include shy, aware of the insecurity and awkwardness often present in my interactions with strangers. But, since arriving abroad, there had been surprisingly little vestige of the shyness I had thought central to my personality. It had been replaced by an undaunted gregariousness. I'd been out and about often, sitting in Bar Prat with my sketchbook or at Café Heidi with my laptop, talking to anyone who would talk to me. I met exasperated Gabriella, whose little brother had decided to move to Ireland after she had gone through a lot to set up a place and bring him over from Venezuela. Then there was Sergio, a stage actor who wrote down all the islands off the coast, what they are known for, and in what order he suggested I visit them.

I phone David, who is immersed in Harlem and writing a blog about what he's discovering in the city and the neighborhood he's adopted from me. He raves about a cafe for its ambience and hospitality. It's two blocks away from my Striver's Row apartment and I'd never even noticed it. We decide to leave each other markers of our time in each other's homes. It's a beautiful suggestion, beautifully put.

I realize, sometimes it takes opening one's eyes wider to see what is right there in front of you.

January 26, 2012 — I fit in with misfits. Two weeks into the trip, though my Spanish had become far less ragged than when I'd arrived, I determined I needed professional help to get further, faster. Nathan recommended a school, and I signed up for a 4-week intermediate language class.

I immediately fell in among my people. They were a hodgepodge cast of characters — two 21-year-old German guys (who are au pairs), two ballerinas (one Russian, one Israeli), a businessman, a student from England, Japanese and Chinese moms, and an ESL teacher from New Orleans — brought together by short-term stints in the country. Our placement test had assigned us to a class for those somewhere beyond beginners but far away from fluent.

We can engage in commerce, tell you where we're from and what we do, and even be one or two story telling guests at dinner parties. But we get lost in quick banter, and ask, "*Como se dice?*" a lot.

We go to language class every day for a couple of hours, and it's a fun time. The instructor is Ana, and every language but Spanish is strictly prohibited. She calls us by country — America, Japan, Israel — and when she puts us in groups, she tells us to play nicely together. Ana says one word in English, "e-stop." Without fail, this is directed at Germany, who perpetually cut up in class.

Today we are practicing the future subjunctive form and are sharing what we would like to do. Someone would like to get out of his marriage when he gets a job that allows him to afford the house payments on his own. We sympathize with all parties involved.

Outside of class, many of us become the most unlikely of friends. The distance usually created by gaps in ages or differences in professions and perspectives pales in comparison to the connections we share through glances across a table, indicating that underneath it all, we have some things intrinsically in common.

January 27, 2012 — I do just fine on my own. I fly to Rome. I am staying at a short-term rental operated by twenty-something-year-old Cecilia. She greets me and sits down at her kitchen table. And in response to, "how are you doing?" says she's not doing well. She and her boy-friend have just split up. I give her a hug, and she bursts into tears. I hold her as she sobs. Heartbreak is the same all over the world.

Out on the street as I walk about, I am confused for being French again. Now I'm thinking that *maybe* I am French, or from some country conquered by the French. I don't know. We don't know. I have a growing desire to try to trace my family's roots back as far as I can.

I try to go see the Colosseum and the Palatine, but they are closed due to a strike. I am not bummed. I think power to the people and take pictures from the outside.

I peek inside a museum, to see some busts. They all look alike. A bust is a bust is a bust.

I discover the biggest danger in Rome is motor vehicle versus pedestrian. There is little regard for the lighted green walking man or the crosswalk. The best way to get across the street is to run. This is what the Romans do, so this is what I do. As they say, 'when in Rome.' I am amused by getting to say this in real-life.

January 28, 2012 — I explore today and yesterday. When I'd emailed one of my oldest college friends and told her about my upcoming trip, she had said it was like "*Eat Pray Love,* with Soul."[xi] But it wasn't quite. I was eating within a pauper's budget, had late-discovered spiritual motivations, and had no intention to and limited experience with having any sort of successful affair. I had come to explore, both what was inside and what was outside.

I go to the Colosseum, the fighting place of the gladiators; the Palatine, the mythical birthplace of the city; the Forum, the hub for conducting government affairs; and the Pantheon, built as a temple for the gods and the oldest intact building.

These four places are 1,800-2,500 years old, and even though some sections are roped off, many areas are not. I walk on marble slabs, climb limestone steps, and sit on chiseled bleachers. I touch my fingertips to cold stone, stroke statues, walk into hidden chambers, and hang over balconies. I fully experience what's right there before me, knowing that I may never come in contact with it again. I am simultaneously part of a particular time and a continuance of a story that's been playing out for thousands of years.

January 29, 2012 — I pray. I am outside of the Vatican. It's the last Sunday of the month, which is the only Sunday the museum is open. And it's open for free. The line starts three city blocks away and winds around in a huge piazza. I wait for hours.

I enter the museum and there are marble statues everywhere — in the courtyards, in display cases, in chapels, lining the walls like bric-a-brac. Frescoes decorate the floor, and chalices made of gold and other precious metals line the shelves. The church feels opulently rich and powerful in a way that makes me cautious. I imagine turning down the wrong hallway, happening upon a secret society conversation, and finding myself disappeared.

I walk through the Galleria delle Carte Geografiche and on the walls are twenty panels of maps of Italy that took the artist three years to complete. But I don't know why anyone looks at anything other than the ceiling. The paintings above are rendered with such depth they look like reliefs. I walk through the hallway twice, one time with my head tilted back and eyes looking only up.

I then find myself in the world-famous Sistine Chapel. Its ceilings and walls ornate with meticulously painted religious portraits. Many have remarked about the painting, but being in the room is an experience unto itself. Two-thousand people can fit at a time, and I gather they are all there.

It looks like the press outside of the Oscars. Cameras are flashing, boom mics are dangling on long metal rods, and shoulder-held TV cameras shoot live footage. People all around are providing information and impressions, condensing the overlap of art and religion into newsworthy sound bites, and engaging in quite poignant and meaningful conversations that seem like they could only happen in that place. They are asking each other what we can and cannot know to be true about our existence as human beings and our place in the divine order. Full of fragments of enlightenment, I walk out into the cobblestone square and light of the day.

Then I get into another line to wait to enter St. Peter's Basilica and attend mass. Mass is fully in Italian, but the components are the same as back home. I stand and kneel and make the sign of the cross on my forehead and on my lips. I pick up lots of the creed, the Lord's Prayer, and bits and pieces of the homily. I say, "Lord, I am not worthy to receive you, but only say the word and my soul shall be healed." We say Amen in unison. And inside a quiet pew, I pray for a long time to be released from my most poignant afflictions. I feel healed.

If you are on your path, you'll feel connected to the outer world and inner world in ways that are seamless and profound.

February 2, 2012 — I see, touch, and taste. Friends, Nicole and Sarah come to visit. Nicole is an about-her-business lady whose classy style is so cinched it's easy to imagine she was a ten-year-old in stilettos running a burgeoning enterprise. Sarah's prim first impression provides canopy for her boisterous inner workings, until she recants a story complete with impressions and everyone falls to the floor laughing. They are both part intelligentsia, part sass, and a little bit of native New York storm come to make landfall in Barcelona. They visit during the four coldest days of the year. The locals say these days happen in February and are adamant there are *only and exactly* four — but that doesn't stop us from living our best lives.

We visit the masterwork of a basilica, La Sagrada Familia, designed by the beloved architect Gaudí. Started over 100 years ago, it is still under construction. The west façade displays the Stations of the Cross, and the south façade depicts the ascension and promises to be the most elaborate. Some say it'll take twenty more years to finish, but there's no telling.

We go on a grand search through the Barri Gòtic (the gothic neighborhood) to find the critically acclaimed and highly recommended Los Caracoles restaurant, but it is closed, so we stand outside and touch our hands to the glass pretending to warm them on the rotisserie chicken in the window.

We find an eatery we can walk in that has all the traditional tapas. Pan Con Tomate — sliced and toasted brioche rubbed with crushed tomato puree. Patatas Bravas — roasted white potatoes cut into irregular cubes and served drizzled with a spicy mayo-based sauce (a staple in every pub). Bombas — stuffed and fried mashed potato balls. Bacalao — dried and salted cod. Pimientos — charred spicy green peppers with salt and olive oil. Tortilla de patata y jamón — mini baked potato quiche with ham. Chocolate con churros — cinnamon and sugar-dusted fried dough sticks accompanied by warm chocolate sauce for dipping.

We overstuff ourselves because we can't bear to leave any of the goodness behind.

February 5, 2012 — I hear. We'd already acted our ages and discovered the Harlem Jazz Club and listened to a small band with a clear and chatty trumpet. We'd gone down to Eixample, where Roser hosted a *pica pica*, a potluck style dinner where there is a little bit of everything to pick on. In between bites of all sorts of cheeses, sausages, mushrooms, spicy shrimp, desserts, and a repeatedly interspersed "Mmmm, what's this?," we heard about Portuguese writer, poet, and essayist, Fernando Pessoa and his multiple literary personalities — three of which wrote thirty-five poems in one night.

Tonight, we club. We head to a venue recommended by a teenaged language school classmate and find the crowd to be mixed in age from 19 to 50. They play top 40, pop, and R&B. I dance carefree and lively to Rihanna's, *We Found Love*, when my attention is commanded by a live violinist who steps into the middle of the dance floor to accompany the chorus. It's one of the most mesmerizing and electrifying sounds I've ever heard, as if all the atoms in the room conspired to produce the refrain. I think this is what hip hop must sound like in heaven.

February 6, 2012 — I ruuuuun. We wake up early and — attracted by a cheap thirty-minute flight and a documentary about major league baseball's Curt Flood, who absconded to the island after railing against the establishment — head to Mallorca for a one-day trip.

When we are on the tarmac, there's an announcement that we have to wait for the plane's wings to be de-iced. After two hours of frustrated waiting, circling the airport, and looping announcements, the other passengers start to chant and whistle and kick the floors until we finally take off.

When we get to the island, it's immediately worth the wait. We visit a real castle, complete with moat and draw-bridge and towers. We go to the Arab bathhouse and sit in the garden surrounded by an elaborate conservatory and a history of revolution and resistance. In a semi-conscious state, in the sun, we all make a pledge that if we ever become ridiculously rich, we'll buy a place in Mallorca. And, if astronomically rich, we'll live in the bathhouse gardens.

We head back to the airport to catch the departing flight. We are there super early and ask if we need to get exit stamps since we were required to get entry stamps. The attendant says no.

We go through the security checkpoint and proceed to chill in the duty-free shop. Sarah performs due diligence to select a fancy bottle of olive oil, thoroughly reading each of the labels, and finally choosing a rare one infused with herbs — processed particularly, and not available for purchase in the U.S.

We walk slowly to the gate from which our flight is set to depart, find three chairs, and leisurely chat while intermittently leaning our tired heads back to sneak moments of shuteye.

Then they make the announcement that we will be boarding and start to call passengers. We are the first to go up. The attendant looks over the first boarding pass, searching. She says it does not have an exit stamp. We explain that we were told we did not need such a stamp. She explains that we, indeed, require one; that the plane will be taking off in twenty minutes; that it is the last plane of the night; and that they will not hold it for us. The kiosk we need to visit is back at the entry to the airport — over a mile there and another mile back, including a trip through security.

We look at each other, look in the direction we need to go, and we start to ruuuuuun.

We run as fast as we can.

We make it to the kiosk. One-by-one we flip our passes down and motion to stamp us. Stamp us quick. Then we turn around and run back, but not without pausing to wave a finger at the attendant.

Running back through the security gate, we bring attention to ourselves, jumping in front of people, delivering quick apologies and truncated explanations that sound like, "Late. We're late." The security guard tells Sarah she cannot bring the olive oil through. With gusto, she throws it into the trashcan and keeps running. I watch from behind as the guard looks to consider detaining her, opts to shrug it off, and lets her keep going.

I run with all I have, but I am the slowest and looking at the others up ahead. The first makes it to the gate, goes left, and is out of sight. Then, the second.

When I get there, the flight attendant is standing next to the door, closing it. She waves me over quickly with a smile, checks the stamp, and as I step through, she closes the door behind me.

We take our seats, dripping with sweat, chests heaving. The other passengers look at us like they are wondering what happened. We laugh so hysterically we're crying; we are grateful to have made it.

When you're on your path, you're checked in to all your senses and sensibilities, and can embrace what they show and tell you about what to do in the moment.

February 8, 2012 — I am part of life's metaphors. Earlier in their visit, we walked through a real-life labyrinth at Parc del Laberint d'Horta. None of us had ever actually been in one. It was more than I had dreamed. An actual maze of ten-foot hedges. We couldn't see over or through them. As we bent around one corner or another, there were choices to make regarding which way to go. We happened upon hidden bunches of bright flowers and out-of-the-way alcoves where teenagers were hiding inside to canoodle, with no intention of emerging for a while. It was light out and there was no chance of coming across weird creatures. And we were traveling through as a merry bunch of friends, so we had not taken navigating all that seriously.

Until we got lost. We walked into a dead end and had to double back, and figure out another way through.

Somewhere between the violin and the labyrinth, I feel like I've lived a full life.

As I'm riding uptown on the metro, after having taken my friends to the airport, I'm content. On the L5 train at Sants Estacio, the train is often crowded, and someone is there entertaining the passengers. But, by the time the train arrives in Horta, the crowd has thinned. There are no more tourists or performers, just regular people, like me, going home.

February 16, 2012 — I like to do business. I have been working remotely on consulting projects for clients in the States, including being a part of the Spank Rock music team. The independent album, *Everything is Boring and Everyone is a F***ing Liar*[xii] had been released in September 2011. I work with the accountants, other artists, collaborators, and management via email. And the team is planning for singles, videos, and tours associated with the album's release.

Today, *Car Song* debuted and is featured in *Rolling Stone Magazine*. I'm communicating with the web designers to get a new splash page up on the site, asking for reconciliations of the budget vs. actuals for a show in Australia, planning for SXSW in May, and corresponding with Alexander Wang's people — the designer is offering garb for the tour.

Instead of the concrete, asphalt, and high buildings of the Big Apple, outside of my window is the understated stucco of a Spanish suburb. To be an international businesswoman, all it had taken was changing where I was seated.

February 26, 2012 — I revel in going back to get things of import. I see the end of the adventure nearing and take to doing all the things I said I would, but hadn't yet. I took the train up to Ribes. I float into the snowy mountains, swinging gently back and forth in a sky lift all to my own, looking down over the whitewashed hills that surrounded me.

I decided to go to carnival in a town that was an hour away. I walked alongside a vibrant parade that had hundreds of different troupes of people dressed in elaborate costume — furry cats, clowns, and headdresses adorned elaborately with feathers.

As dusk comes in, I am still there among a huge and raucous crowd, like at Mardi Gras. No one is there with me and I feel totally fine. Without hesitation, I walk up to strangers to make conversation or ask for suggestions on where to find the best eats. I sit on a low wall by myself and watch the festivities unfold. I am there well into the night. It's something I would have never done before I made the sojourn, but now I feel like I can go just about anywhere and do just about anything.

March 3, 2012 — *I believe in everyday magic.* Over the last couple of weeks, I sat on the sand and sketched, rolled up my jeans, and ran into the ocean. The water was cold and prickly on my legs. I dipped down to put my hands in and collected five seashells for posterity's sake. I had many culminating dinners and drinks and adventures with friends. And I'd sent emails to people stateside asking what they wanted me to bring them back. I was preparing to return.

Nathan had been talking about the *Onion Thing* for weeks. It's a tradition where family and friends gather to roast that season's long green onions on the grill until they are softened and sweet. When they are ready, you dip them in slow-simmered red tomato sauce, and messily slurp them. Folks look forward to it all year.

The final ex-pat gathering is on a rooftop with a subdued and calming view of the city's varied and pastel buildings. The sky is clear, and the wind is gentle. It is by all measures the nicest of days. I go around wishing farewell. A woman from South America tells me I look like a portrait. The flirty Italian in our bunch gives me a kiss on the side of the face.

Then, I take the long roasted onions, dip them, and participate in the slurping. We all laugh at each other's techniques. It is a tender rooftop where cares are free, and there's no agenda but to be in the openness and warmth of friendship.

When Nathan and I leave the party, we go sit together at a restaurant, just us. He gives me one of his drawings; it is red with black swirls. I imagine it as a little bit of romance. I give him one of my drawings with fits of pastel, dragons, and butterflies; it's a little bit a magic.

March 4, 2012 — *I write to remember.* I spend my last night on Carrer San Pere I Miguel, where I started. In my journal, I write: *I have been here for the two months as planned. And Tuesday, at 10:00AM, my flight leaves for New York.*

Remember…this life is yours, not one that belongs to anyone else. You, finally, are not shy. You are pretty…calm, and happy. You make friends — great friends — easily. Everything…is okay.

I am ready to move on. I am ready to be the self I want to be. I want to remember all the moments I sat quietly, with no worries, no agenda, not in a rush to get anywhere.

I write to myself: *Remember the bright Barcelona sunshine on your face…Remember as many of these little moments as possible.*

The Universe not only shows us how we are but *who* we are — who we are in the world at our best.

March 5, 2012 — I find my 'self.' When I first met Nathan and told him my name was Tyette, (pronounced "tie-yet") he responded, "Ah, like a tallat," and explained that in Catalan a tallat (also pronounced "tie-yet") is a small coffee. I hadn't known that.

In the moment, I didn't think much of it other than it being nice to have a phonetic reference with which to introduce myself. It wasn't until the next day when it hit me.

When I was preparing for the trip, if family members asked why I would be overseas for two-months, I would tell them I was going to find myself, and that I thought I might be in a café in Barcelona. This was not a real explanation but was uttered in gest — a shorthand joke that sufficed in lieu of an extended existential explanation of my hippie-like motivations to my not-so-hippie-like kin.

But, in the solitude of the shower, it struck me, and with warm water sheeting down my back, I broke down into a rush of uncontrollable tears mixed with guttural laughter. I marveled at God's magnificent sense of humor and grace.

If a Tyette is a small Catalonian coffee, then I would *literally* find myself in a café in Barcelona. I cried hard, emotion rushing up undeniably from the depth of my soul.

I've waited until today, my last day on the sojourn, to order one. In my favorite café, I ask for a tallat by my name. They bring me a coffee with a pretty picture formed on top,[xiii] and I am found.

This is a dot.

Feel for the Serenity

When the Universe wants us to know we're in the right place at the right time, it sends in a sign, an unmistakably bright one: a dot. A dot is a clear and overwhelming indicator — a confirming message that you have to be in that particular spot at that particular moment to receive.

They are unmistakable and undeniable moments of grace — like that tallat was for me. It was a message sent by the Divine, orchestrated by the Universe to let me know I was on my path, with unmistakable clarity.

The presence of your course markers — your dots — means you're on track, and the absence of them means you're off. They are the beacons of Light on the road that lead *to* and *through* your purpose — what people will say is why you lived, and what you will want to tell God you did with your 'self' and have God agree and be pleased.

A dot glimmers just long enough for you to feel it and confirm that you're going the right way. Then, it is gone, and you keep moving in that direction, remaining open enough to see, hear, and feel the next one.

To find them, *feel.* And ask yourself:

- Who am I?
- Where am I?
- Is this where I'm supposed to be?
- Is this who I'm supposed to be?

And feel for the presence of joy. Joy is not exuberance or relentless cheerfulness. It is a steadiness of the most inner self, a sense of acceptance, balance, gratefulness, and hopefulness. A sense of play. A sense of peace. This is joy. It marks the dots. And the dots light the way.

So…feel for the serenity.
Feel for the calm, the clarity, the joy.
Look for the dots.

CHAPTER 4

A Breakdown in Baltimore

O*ctober 22, 2016* — I am on the other side of a couple of conversations that I hope have put my downward careening to a stop.

I had spent nearly a year falling into a personal crisis. It happened slowly; first, without my realizing it; then without my understanding it; and then without my willingness to recognize and change it. I knew I would have a long and arduous climb back to level ground, where I could feel confident and stand on my feet, because it had taken a while to knock me off of them.

There had been disruption after disruption until I couldn't feel the serenity anymore.

This is the account.

January 21, 2016 — I don't appear to be doing or being enough. My father tells me about a boot on his car. It's a heavy metal clamp-like device that city services installs on a tire to stop a vehicle from moving if the registered owner has aging unpaid parking tickets. He says, "The system put it there." He is typically a gregarious, big-grinned, laughing man, and gifted me with a sense of humor about life, no matter what's going on. We have the same big 'ol, toothy grin, and have spent a lifetime poking well-meaning though sometimes not well-taken fun at circumstances, the weird things other people do, and each other.

We are friends. And as in any other true friendship, there are parts of each other we revere and parts of each other we afford a wide berth of grace. I often combat what I believe is his obstinate cynicism and critical nature. And he is almost always intolerant of my the-world-is-not-out-to-get-you   and   you-are-the-chief-agent-in-your-own-life rationale. Any time I talk like that, he huffs a "Thmph," or chides a "Yeah, yeah," in a my-father-thinks-he-is-a-funny-guy kind of way. This time feels different. He sounds exasperated and disillusioned.

He is angrier than I have ever heard him, yelling about always only having a little bit of money and how badly poor people are treated. I try to cajole him, but in response, he spews out a litany of expletives with expressions of disenfranchisement in between. This is abnormal. I am typically able to soothe my friend.

He says he's going to die soon and asks, "Is this what life is about? Being poor?" I respond, "That's not what life is supposed to be about. It's about the relationships you have along the way." He grumbles a surly affirmation and keeps going with his disdain. He doesn't have time to deal with this, but he has to deal with this. He needs the car to go to work, and he needs to work. He says he's just, "tired of the little people being run over, and tired of the silent majority who sit by and watch it happen." There's a sting inside because even though he doesn't say, I feel somehow he means me. Somehow, I am responsible for the boot on his car. I hear I'm letting my father die poor and tired. I hear, I am disappointing him.

I am sure, out of what feels like nowhere to him, I interrupt mid-sentence. I fire back, "FIIIIIINE, Okay, Okay, Okay. FINE, Okay, I will," mostly responding to what I heard rather than what he actually said. I'm not accomplishing all I can, I hear. I'm wasting what I have been given, I hear.

I say, "FINE. I'll do it. I'll be great," even though I don't know what "great" is — this nebulous, ill-defined, elusive thing that will prove once and for all that I have nothing more to prove. And I don't *actually* want to try at it, but given this conversation, it looks like I must.

I am mad. Living up to my "potential" has been a fruitful yet burdensome part of my life for too long. I thought I had freed myself of it. A few months before, I had said I was letting go of any specific aspirations, that whatever happened moving forward would be "icing," and that what I had already done with my life was enough.

But evidently, it is not. I cannot rest yet. I pick up the mighty burden, which I thought I had laid down.

"Happy?" I say. Then I tell him goodnight and I get off the line.

February 19, 2016 — I can't tell where I'm supposed to be. I leave the office around lunchtime to go to my Uncle Bodie's funeral. I don't tell anyone. I only plan to be out a couple of hours, so I won't have to request time off. I don't feel like explaining our family ties, attempting to fit our connections into the bereavement policy, or going through the exercise of proving the definition of family in the policy inadequate.

He was someone I adored. He had always greeted me with the sincerest of smiles, tender hugs, and drew me in to offside intellectual conversations I could tell he couldn't have with most. To some he was this drug king pin, gangster turned fictionalized TV character on *The Wire*.[xiv] To me, he was a kindred spirit with a personality so complex it was an exclusion from the curve. An outlier. He told me once, "I'm so proud of you. When I was in the pen, I told a lot of [bruhs] in there I had a niece that was at Stanford." It made me proud to make him proud.

When I get to the mosque, I mill around in the front until people I know arrive in long black cars, and then I slunk over and integrate with them gently, imposter-like. I had missed the viewing the night before, having stayed late at work completing a grant proposal that seemed critical.

My job still feels new and what I am tasked to do seems important. I am also being invited to be a part of in-circles and networks in a way unlike any other time in my life. Earlier in the month, I had been at a café with one of the largest builders of commercial real estate in the country. We had apple pie and ginger carrot soup, while discussing the beginning details of a partnership to develop a community-use space that would be offered to non-profit organizations, free of cost. I had first felt imposter-like there too, trying to be chill and come across as if I'd previously been at a table like that, discussing something important like that, with a fancy-person like that. I had not. And by the time the meeting was over, I had been excited and relieved to have gone from thinking I didn't belong at such a table to feeling like I did.

I'm not thinking about any of that at the mosque. I sit in the back rows with the women, looking at the closed casket in front of the room.

I have missed seeing my uncle.

A member of the mosque calls the service to order. The Imam leads the congregation in chanting the Janazah funeral prayer, which is a request for forgiveness and mercy, and a rite of the dead. The singing ends. The service is over.

At the cemetery, the men pick up shovels and throw mounds of dirt over the casket until the hole is filled. The women are invited to participate. I bend down and grab soil with my bare hands and sprinkle it over my uncle and wish him a teary-eyed, belated goodbye.

At the repass, my cousin tells me about how many folks had been at the viewing. She says it was like a reunion of the projects. Hundreds of people had lined up outside the funeral home to get a glimpse of him. There had been drama. Either a purse was stolen at the viewing or a purse was stolen twenty years ago. A fight had broken out between the parties involved (in either the recent theft or the twenty-year-old one, depending on which it was), and the viewing had to be shutdown. I smile. Of course it did, I think. These are my rag-tag, rabble-rousing people and this is how it goes. I conjure the scene in my head.

She says I should have seen Uncle Bodie. She says, "He looked gentle, like a baby with fine, paper soft skin." I would have liked to have seen him like that, so I could remember him on the outside the way I remember him on the inside. I am deeply disappointed in myself.

I go back to the office. I don't tell anyone where I have been.

March 21, 2016 — I am sharing what's not yet sorted. About a thousand people are simultaneously participating in small-group conversations happening all over Baltimore City. The goal of this dinner and dialogue event is to bring together strangers who would not have met otherwise, encourage people to be open and to get to know one another in a way they typically wouldn't. And to leave with relationships that would continue beyond the evening.

I am a facilitator and aided by prompts and questions, we are going to tell our stories. Facilitators have been trained to aid the dialogue, respond to comments, and toggle the floor between participants in a way that everyone feels included. I am supposed to create a safe space by modeling my own vulnerability. It has not been my style to share intimate details of my life. It's hard to know which parts and pieces I want to bring forward, which insider facts I want to reveal, or what I want to expose about my inner workings. I don't know who of me is welcome.

I tell them about my first memories of the police. I was around four when they raided our house. Out of nowhere, there was a loud bang and crash at the door, then barking and teeth coming up at me. I scurried in reverse, screaming and climbing up the back of the couch, trying to get away, when the dog's teeth abruptly stopped coming directly at my face. The dog had turned left sharply, toward the back bedrooms, having been pulled hard by a man in black holding the leash.

It had taken me well into adulthood to get over my fear of and dislike for the police. With Mike Brown and Sandra Bland, I report I am scared of them again.

We go around sharing things it would typically take years to share. We gasp at some sharings. We nod in affirmation at others. We laugh. We cry. We look around at the end and feel like we know each other. What I shared is true, and it feels incomplete.

April 27, 2016 — I am not okay. My friend asks, "Are you okay?" Cassandra is sage-like, grounding, and guiding. "When I talked to you the other day, you didn't sound right," she says. I respond with, "No, I don't think I am." She is stayed by this response. I am at least conscious of whatever it is she hears in my voice, but she will continue to check in. Previously, I'd talked to my friend Jensie, who is unparalleled in her ability to interpret and reflect back. We talked about metamorphosis, and the ugly, painful part of change; how on the way from legs to wings, butterflies find themselves temporarily in the forms of skinless, gooey globs, likely unaware of what will happen next. I feel I'm going through something, but I don't know quite what that something is.

May 5, 2016 — I am surrounded by worry. I worry mostly about the weather. It's changing very drastically in unsettling and predictive ways. It feels like very few are noticing or talking about it. I worry about my father. He's getting older and still traveling around the country to work on construction sites. He crawls into underground pipes, pulling heavy wires through, while wearing a fire retardant suit, because things explode in those holes. He walks on scaffolds hundreds of feet high wearing layers of mountain climbing gear, because people can go hypothermic in wintertime winds. I worry about the country going into war. I worry about the salvation of my soul. I worry that I am worrying so much.

May 16, 2016 — I am almost hyperventilating. The quarterly Board Meeting starts in less than five minutes, and I'm due to present the financial report. It's a big meeting — one that will determine the organizational budget for the next year. I'm in the bathroom taking heaping breaths and pulling myself together. I'm wiping dripping sweat from my face.

Only a half-hour before the meeting was set to start, I'd made the last formatting changes to the multi-paged, graphed, and colored materials, which included last quarter's budget and expenses and next year's projections. In thirty minutes, I needed to print, collate, and package the reports; gather them in an organized pile; and carry them across campus to the meeting room. I had run in high heels with the teetering pile in my hands, made it up the stairs and into the room, placed the packets on the table, and retreated to the bathroom before anyone could get a good look at me.

In the ladies' room, I am taking the three minutes I have left to get composed. I breathe and wipe, breathe and wipe, keeping conscious of time; but not too conscious, because I am sweating and pressure causes more sweat beads to form, and I need them to go away. I breathe and wipe, breathe and wipe, trying to slow down my inhalations and exhalations, and feel for a decrease in my heart rate. I breathe and wipe and breathe and wipe until my forehead is clear. I apply blot powder. Then lipstick. I look put together. Just at the time I'm supposed to be in there, I walk slowly into the meeting room, so no one will notice the heel I'd broken. I smile the warmest smile I have. I grab some of the working dinner that has been laid out and engage in easy chitchat with everyone until the meeting is called to order. When it's time, I'm called up, and I present the financials with the mask of poise that is required.

June 26, 2016 — I am forgetting things. My Aunt Gu and I attend church almost every Sunday together. Raised Catholic, we grew up in different decades attending St. Gregory's in Gilmore Homes. It was right next to the low-rise public housing units of Pressor Court, where Ms. Gloria watched all three of my Grandmother Patsy P's little girls be born — my mother and her two sisters — then welcomed me as the first grandkid. Ms. Gloria still volunteers at the church pantry some forty years later.

Growing up, the church had been a community mainstay — the priest himself would collect up guns when the city did its no questions asked buy back. The church would pay delinquent light bills if parishioners needed, and members would march around the neighborhood on Palm Sunday giving out green palm to anyone who wanted the symbol of renewal.

But a few years ago, the priest we had both grown up with passed away, no one permanent had been placed with our congregation, and some parishioners had gone to different churches to attend service. Gu and I landed in a congregation that was quite a bit more pale and austere than the community we'd left. But the people were nice, and the priest was relatively progressive, so we stayed.

We'd been there for about a year, but we hadn't made any friends or participated in any activities outside of mass. Every week I'd tell myself I was going to do something low-stakes to try to integrate more, so when the annual church picnic was advertised, I wanted to go. Every Sunday prior to the picnic, I'd reminded myself to make a dish to share.

But on picnic day, I walk up to the church steps, watching other parishioners carrying pans. My hands are empty. I have forgotten. We attend mass and leave right before the picnic starts, walking quickly enough, so no one asks us to stay.

When you're in trouble, it's palpable, even before you know exactly what kind of trouble you're in.

July 5, 2016 — I am scared of them because they are scared of us. The cops kill a Black man in Baton Rouge, Louisiana.

81

His name is Alton Sterling. I don't know him, but I know many people like him. I see a man like him regularly, selling CDs. They call him, "The CD Man."

In the media, I see Alton's smiling pictures and hear from the mother of his children. I watch his 15-year-old son break down while speaking of the loss of his father.

I know intrinsically and deeply without any doubt that he was just a regular guy. A CD man is not dangerous. He can't be. He must talk to people and be friendly in order to sell his CDs. He's a salesperson, not a predator. And he's not doing anything but hawking music. That's all. Everyone knows this.

I think the police find even this type of guy threatening. So threatening that rounds are fired at close range into his chest while he is already on the ground. They are scared of us, I think. I think, we are inhuman to them; they swat us like flies.

July 7, 2016 — Nowhere is safe. A woman calls in to the radio station. She says she's a 25-year-old single mother living near Pennsylvania Avenue in Baltimore, and she just doesn't feel safe. She doesn't feel safe with the citizens, she doesn't feel safe with the police, and she doesn't know what to do. She hangs up.

July 8, 2016 — The body I wear feels like a target. I hear about Philandro Castile. He was shot by the police in

Minnesota while it got streamed live. We are under attack, I think. I think, we are under attack.

July 9, 2016 — I run out of good times. My husband and I attend the 9:15PM showing of *Finding Dory*, which I really want to see. It's the sequel to the classic Disney-Pixar animated gem, *Finding Nemo,* about a clown fish on a journey with a hilarious good friend, making his way across an ocean. It's the kind of story that speaks to many parts of me — the little girl I did not leave behind, the journey-maker, and the lover of laughter. My goofing-around repertoire even includes doing an impression of the friend, Dory, attempting to speak whale. Seeing the movie is supposed to be a good, fun and joy-finding time, but I'm already anxious about movie theaters. There have been too many mass shootings and other violent attacks on the public.

After the movie starts, I'm waiting for the uneasy feeling to subside as I get immersed in the cartoon, but then a single white man comes in. He goes to sit down, but he looks at the ceiling, at the walls — everywhere but the screen. He leaves, and then he returns. Again, he leaves and returns. The people behind me lean forward and ask us if he is acting weird. I say yes. They get up and leave, I assume to get security. The man doesn't come back.

It takes some time to steady my heartbeat and ease into the film again. When I do, a different young man walks in and looks around. A second later, two young women wearing hijabs enter and join him. Then three more people join the group. They could just be teenagers, movie hopping. Or this could be the beginning of something terrible. I don't wait to find out. I lean over to my husband and say, "let's leave." He asks if I'm serious. I am. I say, "I can't." I pick up my purse and walk out. We exit the theater and the building. I am so scared. I am ashamed for so many reasons.

July 12, 2016 — I tend in our suffering. I go to Josh's funeral. He's the uncle of my twenty-one-year-old little cousin. I've helped to raise her from birth. It is a sad affair. The story makes the news. Josh had just graduated from Bowie State University with a B.A. A couple weeks later, he was fatally shot driving through a Baltimore neighborhood. There were no leads for the shooting.

The closed casket is placed in the middle of the aisle next to the family pew. Josh's father pulls the casket close to him and strokes the fabric draped over it, as if it is his son's back.

I watch my cousin from across the aisle. She was extremely close to her uncle. She's slunk over in the pew, quietly sobbing, shoulders heaving up and down, legs shaking. She folds into herself, putting her head into her lap. The preacher is delivering the sermon, and he is in the middle of his words. We are not supposed to move, but I pop up and squeeze out of my seat, hurry across the aisle, and squeeze into hers. I hold her as she sobs. Heart break is the same all over the world.

July 16, 2016 — I fight for the survival of home. I married in to six children. They range from five to twenty-years-old. The oldest lives on her own with a roommate, the others live with their moms but frequently spend time with us. I own three houses: one is that first row house that's now being rented out to tenants, one is the multi-unit that me and my husband and my sister and her husband live in, and the third is one I used the equity in the second house to purchase and am renting out to my cousin. We are still renovating parts of some of the properties.

I want to become an extreme couponer. I saw a television show about it years ago and now have a way in because Aunt Gu's new neighbor does it. She will help get the coupons and show me how.

I have also started baking, inspired by my new last name.

In the span of seven minutes, I rework the title of a writing project, tend to a five-year-old (who is in a bubble bath not washing up and not ready to get out), lift a dozen still-cooling homemade cookies off parchment paper so they don't stick, and steam the bottom of a white and pink dress (that said five-year-old will wear outside if she ever gets out of the tub).

In the span of an hour, I bake oatmeal cookies from scratch (with cranberries, cardamom, white chocolate chips, and two old bananas from the top of the refrigerator), give the five-year-old blue berries and pumpkin seeds and chocolate pudding, grab household and home improvement receipts from my husband, write a check so we can settle the accounts, pull out art supplies for a project (paper, markers, fuzzy balls, and glue), visit with our twenty-year-old who was riding by our house on the way to her second job, and chat about what I am doing with my hair.

Within the span of three hours, I journal a couple thousand words, meet with the window man and have him scope out the panes to be replaced, water the plants, bid "see you later" to our two boys who had stayed over the night before, do some totaling of expenses, read an article on writing, read a quick story about political candidates choosing their running mates, see stories of the horrible attack in Nice, France (where a 19-ton cargo truck was driven purposefully into a crowd celebrating Bastille Day, killing 86 and injuring 456[xv]), opt not to read more news, call my aunt to see if she'd received the stacks of coupons I'd ordered, and prep a list of the groceries and household products I will buy with said coupons, once clipped.

July 19, 2016 — I am beside myself with helplessness. I am visiting with my father. It has been our tradition every year to go to Artscape together. It's one of the largest public festivals in the nation. Thousands of people attend. Within a couple dozen blocks of roped off streets, there are multiple stages with musical performances by mega artists and artisanal local bands, short-term one-storied sculptural installations, a row of elaborately decorated cars, every edible fried object, and hundreds of artists displaying and selling their wares — paintings, furniture, earrings, melted beer bottles turned into working clocks, and forks welded into marsupials and arachnids.

I've been drawing since I was a toddler and painting more seriously since college. My mother was a talented artist; it's one of the gifts she passed on to me, and it makes me feel more whole to have part of her within.

My father and I are both arts aficionados, and we love to go together and clamor over whatever strikes us.

Before we are set to go to the festival, I arrive at his house and we spend time in his garden. He had started gardening several years before by turning over the soil in an abandoned lot adjacent to a mechanics garage and making it fruitful with colorful peppers, leafy greens, and tomatoes.

He now has a small plot in his backyard, which backs to an alley. I ask if the city rats come in to eat the produce. He says they don't like vegetables; they only want to eat chicken boxes. My father tells me to take the cherry tomatoes; he's grown way too many. He and I reach into and under the leaves and branches of the bushes to get them. I pick all the ripe ones, by first doing a gentle test pull to see if they are loose, and then plucking them from and vine and placing them in a bag; maybe seven pounds. It's hard work, hot and sticky. And we've only been out there twenty minutes, and we're well fed, hydrated, and there of our own free will.

We look at each other. We are thinking about the slaves. We speak of them, our people, and lament their lot. We enter a sobering conversation about the state of America and from where this state was born. It's a nation struck up on the backs, brutalized bodies, broken bones, and betrayed spirits of my ancestors. And still we are in the struggle.

He says he doesn't want to go to ArtScape. He doesn't want to leave the house. He's a 55-year-old Black man, and he feels in danger everywhere. He wants to stop going to cookouts with his friends from work, where he is the only person of color, because those have become places that can potentially turn hostile. He's concerned that the police will stop him in his car, because those interactions can be deadly. And he can't go into the hood because, "the young dudes are crazy." He can't go anywhere. My father tells me he feels trapped. He just wants to stay home.

I don't know what I can do.

July 20, 2016 — I am neglecting and avoiding. My mortgage is overdue. I have the money, but I haven't sent in the payment. I miss a required housing inspection for a rental property. I owe friends responses to personal emails. I have become unresponsive to some emails at work, most saliently, the ones about the audit. It's been four weeks since I've opened my snail mail or listened to my voicemail. The unopened mail is a canary in a coalmine. I say I must open it all, but only get through two pieces.

July 26, 2016 — I am trying to push through. It's twenty-five minutes before my birthday. I've managed to open my paper mail over the last few days, and as a present to myself, I want to have listened to all of my still unretrieved voicemail messages before the clock strikes midnight. I say to myself ready, set, go, but then spend eleven minutes getting blue cheese and crackers, putting on my bedclothes, and pouring seltzer water.

With fourteen minutes left, I think I must…**go**…now.

I dial in to the mailbox. It says, "Your mailbox is full. Please delete some of your messages." I have *36* new ones. I press 1 to listen.

The initial voices are familiar. The first three messages are from my father, saying hi or asking me to call him. There's a message from Cassandra checking in. I keep going. Several are from the alarm company, indicating a fault on one of the alarm systems that I need to tend to. I press 1, 1, 1, 1, 1, 1 to get through the messages left by the robo-dialer.

The gas and electric company has called with customer alerts about power outages in the area. I continue to press 1. There's a message from a colleague who'd already followed up with an email. 1. The dentist called with a reminder for an appointment I'd already attended. 1. The window guy. 1. Someone about the rental property. 1. Home Depot. 1, 1, 1, 1. My Aunt. A girlfriend of mine. Another from Daddy. Granny. 1, 1, 1, 1.

Four minutes before my birthday, I've cleared a month's worth of voicemail.

I sit on the floor a minute and pray.

August 10, 2016 — I want to scream. What it feels like to be me in America right now is to always be on the thin-lined cusp, the ungated precipice, the quivering verge of uncontrollably releasing, violently purging, operatically effusing…a mighty, guttural, wailing, blood-curdling, memory-obviating, tear-drenched, battle-crying, motherly scream. And then, when everyone has been mesmerized under the paralytic boom of the reverberating sound, and is quieted and paying full attention, to want to say "enough."

August 26, 2016 — I run out of words. It's before 8:30AM, and I am in a high octave, rigorous, hyped-up conversation with my husband, mad about some worky thing at work. It is not easy to manage the operations components of a business and consistently try to be open and vulnerable, even when that's what you've signed up to try to do. Nor is it a non-thing to know if I release what's below the veil without coding it in a way that's relatable to a broader audience[xvi] that it may not be consumed in a way that's constructive.

So, I let it out at home.

A litany of words are gushing out. Until they aren't.

I start to stumble. To stutter. I try to speak, but the words are chopped up. I attempt a "D" sound, but it comes out as a "G."

I become fearful about what is happening as my brain catches up to what is and *is not* coming out of my mouth. I look at my husband to see if he has noticed. I attempt the next sound but my lips are askew from the words in my head as if the sound and the display on a screen have become unsynced, and the sound is uncontrollably going in and out of mute.

I suck in multiple short bursts of air in a row, and then can force out a slow sentence with a lengthy pause between each word.

"I............can't............talk."

He turns his eyes up and looks at me inquisitively. We exchange more looks and gestures as we're trying to work out with each other what's going on. I try to push out more sounds, but my brain is still disconnected from my mouth and mostly "gah" and "fuh" stutters come out. I take in more breaths and manage "hospital."

We jump in the car. On the way, I'm able to say a thing here or there, but very slowly. Mostly I'm silent and thinking that if I am having a stroke, how mad I am going to be.

Very mad. (Much madder than my father was about the boot.)

I think of how *not* apropos it would be if someone who says as much as me couldn't talk. My defiant insides immediately resist. I think I will get one of those machines where I type and it speaks. I shake my head at my internal response to the circumstance and manage to find a little room to laugh inside the fear. But just a little.

We get to the emergency room. I'm starting to push consonants back together with their appropriate sounds, smooth out words and form sentences. I've gone from not being able to say much of anything to needing to think and calm down and speak very slowly.

We tell the triage nurse my symptoms. They skip me through check-in and I am taken straight to a room, where nurses and doctors surround me quickly. They hook me up to monitors and an IV. Tests begin. I follow their fingers with my eyes and look at the flashlight shined in them. They test my motor skills and reflexes. They ask me what my name is and who the president is. I give urine and blood samples. I have an MRI and a CAT scan. The day passes in the hospital. Everything comes back normal. I am talking normally again.

The physician says whatever was happening was an episode of "aphasia," which can be caused by a number of things. None of the tests give any indication of stroke or preliminarily point to a medical cause, but I need to go to my primary care doctor and run down why it happened.

In my mind, I already know why: stress. I'm already calling it a breakdown. A breakdown caused by good old, garden variety, underestimated, can-lead-to-the-psych-ward, can shut-down-the-body's-functions, can-definitely-kill stress.

We go home.

September 12, 2016 — *I feel my insides.* I'm at the lady doctor and she says my uterus is the size of someone who is five months pregnant, which I am not. Over the last year, I have gained weight and noticed my protruding belly. My husband had pressed on it, felt its firmness, and said I needed to see the doctor. I hadn't.

The need to tend to my own body had been displaced. But when I ended up in the emergency room, they had asked questions about how I was feeling, and about what in my body hurt, and those questions had made me notice how much did, *actually*, hurt. After the emergency room visit, I had decided to set up appointments I had been neglecting, to get myself checked out.

I am seeing the gynecologist. She feels around my abdomen and says there are masses. I had been told years before that I had fibroids. At the time I learned of them, the benign tumors were small and asymptomatic and the recommendation was to leave them alone.

She says the masses could be those fibroids having grown, or a rare form of uterine cancer. She says this flatly with practiced, slow pacing. She doesn't sound worried, but she doesn't sound not worried. I must go for ultrasound and send her the results when they come back.

September 14, 2016 — *I am getting cut into.* I am laying on a paper sheet and a doctor is cutting my scalp, after having jabbed me several times with a long needle to numb the skin. There is no pain, but I can hear the snips of the surgical scissors and feel the pressure of her digging around, scoring.

I am balding.

My hair has been thinning out at the top of my head for years, and I've finally gone in to see a dermatologist about it. She says it's probably Alopecia. She shows me pictures of the worst progressions, where women have ended up with hair dusted on parts of their scalp, or with shiny large portions of bald skin where the hair follicles have died. She shows me these after she says the disorder itself is relatively common but degenerative if not treated. The pictures are what can happen over time if it's not addressed early enough. To treat it — with medicated cream, prescription shampoo, and months of repeated visits to get injections into the top of the head — she's got to definitively diagnose it. That means getting a quarter-sized flap cut into my scalp and a pen-point sized piece of flesh excised so it can be sent to the lab.

In our disquieted places, there are realizations — tough truths that shadow in the road and confirm we are in a perilous spot.

September 16, 2016 — *I am still running.* A conversation with my best friend Cruz, starts with his asking why I'd been so late at work given all that's going on. For twenty years, we've been having authentic exchanges unconstrained by any semblance of need to be politically correct. He's the one who offered that mattress on a floor in Brooklyn.

I tell him some of what I'm working on and he says, "That sounds like a lot of pressure."

I then remind him I am signed up to run a 5K in about a month. He says something akin to, "You're being stupid." Though running in the 5K has become a tradition for me, my husband, and the family, to honor his mother who passed away from cancer, Cruz doesn't think running is a good idea given how spent I sound. He says, "Sit down. You're done." And threatens to come down from New York and get me if I don't start acting right.

"I want to cry."

"Okay," he says, "cry. But sit the fuck down and cry, because you are done running."

But I don't listen.

September 19, 2016 — I see everything almost burn down. My father texts and says he's seeing it on the news, right then, that the house next to mine is on fire. I text back asking if it's the one "Attached?!" I rush to the scene. When I get to my street, the block is completely shut down with fire trucks and police. The hydrants are open and water is being projected onto the buildings. I get closer. Yellow tape is around three houses: mine on the right, a neighbor's on the left, and the one in the middle — which is the one that caught fire.

On the roof and inside the second floor, the firemen are working. The windows are busted out and everything is black and smoldering. The firemen spray the hose and rip out pieces of the structure. It looks like they are not sure if the fire is done or if the flames are still moving inside the walls. They are trying to stop it from spreading. They take chunks of wood, rafters, and walls and throw them from the second floor, onto the concrete below. They spray water and look to be digging into the walls and throwing chunks to the ground, more and more toward my house. Eventually they slow and then they stop. The fire is out. My house is still intact.

October 9, 2016 — I am over-tired and still going. Our neighbor's home was devastated. She moves in with her family while there's a plan made for repair. Our roof sustained some damage, and the rafters took a lot of smoke and soot. But the inside of our house — apart from firemen's footprints and a few smudgy handprints on the walls — was relatively untouched.

On the day of the fire, the American Red Cross showed up right away to make sure we had food and a place to sleep for the night. Then the home insurance company put us up in a long-term hotel. We needed to be displaced out of our house for weeks. Every piece of clothing we owned needed to be dry-cleaned, the structure needed to be repaired, and air needed to be filtered — it smelled as if the whole place had been barbequed. The soot needed to be removed, and the entire inside of the house repainted.

I had been dealing with the insurance claims and the services and construction contracts.

I have also been awash in projects at work. On Friday, I left the office after six pm feeling too tired and wanting to talk about it. I called Cruz, but he hadn't answered. I called my dad, but he was heading to a wake for a friend who had been killed in an attempted robbery. I called my husband, but he hadn't picked up. I stopped calling and drove to the supermarket to shop, because there wasn't any real food in the hotel room.

Now I am writing a speech I am set to give soon at the Women of the World Festival. The speech isn't ready. I have not practiced and I need to be on stage in less than two hours.

I take too long in the shower. I put on my dress and my open-toed shoes and my mascara. I pick up my computer and my bag. I put the half-written speech inside. I will have to finish and practice there. I head toward the event.

When the world doesn't stop, the Universe tries to tell you that it's you who needs to.

October 20, 2016 — I scream for help. I am dreading an unread email. I forget the finance call. I dial my sister.

Feel for the Disruption

Dots are the Universe's way of letting us know we're going the right way, but they are not the way the Universe tells us we're going the wrong way. When we're in trouble, the Universe tries to guide through disruption — the lack of calm, the absence of clarity, the dearth of joy. Sometimes these moments feel like distraction or dissonance — my forgetting the church picnic or feeling like I was going through something but not knowing what. And sometimes these disruptive moments are acute and intense — wanting to scream or rushing to the emergency room because I couldn't speak.

And while we deal with our own introcosms[xvii] and face challenges in our microcosms — a problem at work, health concerns, a house fire — we are not insulated from the macrocosms — climate change, an unstable political situation, a tense social environment.

We exist on earth, in cities, in families, in communities, and in societies. We have to deal with ourselves and with everything else. At the worst of times, the maze is an unpredictable, messy, scary one — one that sometimes only appears to be dangerous and sometimes actually is. That's what makes it difficult to listen in times of disruption, but we must.

A former-colleague and friend, Jen Trepanier, suffers from an autoimmune disease that has put her in harm and pain's way since she was a teenager. She now helps people find wisdom within suffering. She leads an initiative that matches puppies, who benefit from socialization before being placed into permanent homes, with medically ailing children. The children and their families get to spend uninterrupted time cuddling furry cuteness and experiencing the healing power of joy. Jen speaks often of balance, about not just taking the bad with the good, but within suffering, seeking out the good that can only be discovered there. She says, "Within darkness, there is Light" and encourages us to see what gifts our toughest times bring. That requires leaning in to the moment and listening, so you can hear the messages that may only be present there.

When I was on my way to breakdown, I had gotten troubled on a troubled road. But instead of noticing my pain and sitting still, I kept going. So, the Universe kept speaking over and over. There was disruptive moment after disruptive moment, until I finally heard, and stopped and looked for a way out. Who knows what damage would have been caused if I hadn't.

So…feel for the disruption.
When you find yourself in trouble, it's time to pay the most attention, to stop and look in the direction of the Light.

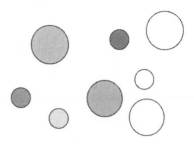

CHAPTER 5

Finding Your Path

March 6, 2012 — I am sitting on the flight back from Spain, full of insights and scratching them down in my journal as fast as they come to mind.

I had barely made the plane.

Having misjudged the time needed to travel to the airport, I barrel out of the taxi and hand my bags hurriedly to the curbside check-in attendants. They tell me they will take them even though I might not make the flight. I nod, turn toward the sliding doors, and…I run.

Having been to the airport to pick up my friends, I remember where to find the electronic board that lists departure and arrival gates. I run there, glance for a milli-second to get the details, and then keep running.

I am leveraging tangible and intangible takeaways from the sojourn and applying findings gathered along the way.

I sprint faster than the previously prudent parts of my adult form would have allowed. I had sheathed a particular brand of self-consciousness on the very first day in Barcelona, when I had to say all kinds of wrong words to strangers trying to find that electrical adaptor. And I had learned, quite poignantly from the airport experience in Mallorca.

In my heart and in my gut is an intense understanding.

Even when you're on your path, sometimes you have to run. You have to run like the doors are closing.

I careen down the slippery airport lengths. I make a sharp turn where the monitor said, and I see the check-in counter and the entrance to the corridor I need, where departure gates are. No one is in line. It looks like all the passengers have gone down the ramp that leads to the other section of the airport. One staffer is clicking a rope into place to indicate that it's too late to pass. And another attendant is placing a closed sign on the counter. I jolt up and ask if there's any way she can let me through.

She says no. She's sorry, but boarding is closed. I explain as best and as quickly as I can, that I am trying to get home. I put it all on the table with a genuine, "please." The staff person standing next to her looks at me empathetically and then looks at her and says with a little nod, "Let her through."

I give an emphatic thank you, get my ticket stamped, rush by the ropes, and continue to run to the plane.

I make it.

From my seat, I write, *God is good…Push. Run. Be Kind. Keep trying, and the doors might be open.* I am grateful for the kind soul who kept the way open for me and remind myself to be kind to someone else.

The Universe asks us to be thankful for the gifts we receive, and to put goodness back out into the world for others.

For the rest of that flight I think of my journey, what I learned, and about the person I'd discovered and rediscovered I was.

When I get back to Harlem, I know I'm going to leave New York. And, two days after I've come back from Spain,

I'm sitting in my studio apartment thinking about next steps. I've reached the end of my savings runway, and first things first, I say out loud, "I need to get a job." And by that afternoon, believe it or not, an old friend and colleague — from the organization that I had been at before I took the gap-year — calls. She's now the head of the department, and she needs someone right away to be temporary Assistant Vice President.

This is a dot.

By bringing forth exactly what you need, right when you need it, the Universe is letting you know you are in the right place.

I had gone to Barcelona to find myself — and by way of tallat, I literally had. I had also learned my favorite poem, "Listen to the Mustn'ts,"[xviii] and all it means to me, by heart. I had learned to cook well enough, and even to grill chicken by stovetop and make pancakes from scratch. I had learned that I really like soup, but I really do not like mayonnaise — even when it is mixed with other ingredients and slathered on top of crispy potatoes. I learned to speak conversational Spanish. That I draw. That I am no longer shy. That I make friends easily. That I'm in for doing the work, but have no traditional career aspirations (which turns out to be a whole 'nother story).

I had also come to define my 'self'. When I am at my best, *I am a part of wherever here is, recognize change, and seek family. I am worldly, lulled by the blues, and inspired by art. I believe in the law of attraction, get along with the even thoughs, look to grow in my awareness, fit in with misfits, and do just fine on my own. I explore today and yesterday. I pray. I see, touch, and taste. I hear. I ruuuuun. I am part of life's metaphors, like to do business, and revel in going back to get things of import. I believe in everyday magic. I write to remember. And I'm always seeking to find my 'self'.*

A large part of the trip had also been about figuring out exactly where home was. I had done that by paying attention to what I missed, what I did not miss, and therefore, what home should have and be like.

I missed…my father. When we were stateside, I frequently gave him the chiding hard time any good-friend / eldest child gives, and when he was far away, I missed our banter and being so close. I missed my funny, zany, dance-crazy, uber-smart, accomplished, sassy girlfriends and the Y-chromosomed advisors who often saved us from the many things we'd come up with when left to our own devices. I missed my family (which is just so crazy and loud that the rest of the world often seemed noticeably quiet), and my babies in particular (the little cousins and Goddaughter who were in high school, middle school, and elementary school then). They had visited me in New York, rode those rides at Coney Island too, and are coming along behind us on the road we tread. *I missed* movies and food served really hot (which it rarely was in Spanish restaurants). I missed the swipe feature on my cell phone, strong water pressure, my hairdresser, Sriracha, and the things I had not yet discovered where I lived. *I did not miss*...snow or anything else cold falling from the sky, television, election coverage, or noise in or trash on the streets. *I would miss*...being so close to the sea, good produce at good prices, cheap beer and wine, writing almost every day, and the good company of kind-hearted, blue-eyed nomads, traveling ballerinas, and their kindred — citizens of the world, opening up their arms, hearts, and communities freely, because they seem to know and practice intrinsically what it takes others a long time to get: we all belong.

That meant that home needed to have soup, did not necessarily need a television, and required that the seashore not be too far away. And, most importantly, needed to have easy access to my people.

And so, I followed the dots home.

I would spend the next six months filling that temporary role, wrapping up my affairs, and wishing a farewell to New York and that stage in my life with all the honor, fanfare and gratitude it deserved. Then I would be on a train headed south. Having run away years before, I would be pointed back in the direction of Baltimore.

Cherish Your Journey Mates

One of the ways I most knew I was where I was supposed to be was by who was with me, and what joy, wonder, love, and enlightenment we brought to each other. While you are traveling through the maze, you are not alone. You have family. You have co-workers. You have partners. You have fans. You have friends. You have journey mates.

Sometimes they are people with whom you have life-long relationships. Sometimes they are people who come into your life for a season. And sometimes they are strangers in passing who do something for you that you could not do for yourself — like the skydiving instructor who strapped herself to my back and worked the parachute so I could experience the glory of the sky, and the airport attendant who let me through the closed gate.

I met my best friend, Cruz, in college. It was a tradition to ambush other students with water blasters. When my dorm had rushed in to surprise first years from another dorm, they were waiting for us. We fled across campus with them in fast pursuit. I had seen Cruz before, but didn't know him. We happened to duck into the same empty room to hide under a table, while the other students came rushing by, looking for us. After a few minutes, when the footsteps died down, I moved to get up and leave. He put his hand on my arm to have me sit back down. So I waited. It was the first, but not the last time he'd tell me to sit the bleep down. Twenty years later, he'll tell you he saved me from getting up too fast, being discovered, and being drenched. I will tell

> *"Never leave a friend behind. Friends are all we have to get us through this life*
> *-and they are the only things from this world that we could hope to see in the next."*
>
> Dean Koontz

you I saved him, because he was out of breath, and needed more time to recover. We've been friends ever since. We won't ever know who saved who that first time, but we know we are on this journey together.

In Barcelona, I found the expatriate, transient, and no-madic communities quickly, and we were one. There was Chen, the beautiful, Israeli traveling ballerina and songstress who I met in Spanish class and who became my most frequent and closest girlfriend. We sat across from each other at many a table chatting of romance and family and dreams. She taught me how to slow-roast cauliflower by explaining that I had to "burn" it because that was the closest English word she knew to use. She played a "spe-cial" song for me once that I still listen to many years later and remember with what care and intention she walked across the room and put it on. And there was Jean Emile, a renowned and talented dancer who became a ballet instructor and choreographer. Like a dream, he let me sit in on his class to sketch ballerinas like Degas did. I got to be in the best seats at a burlesque show he choreographed at El Molino, a replica of the Moulin Rouge. The show had a rendition of Beyonce's, *Put a Ring On It*, aerial feats, and a cheeky, terribly funny traditional Spanish song about Vaseline. He was from Harlem, had been living abroad for years — not just in Spain but in the Netherlands and in Italy — and shared with me the many things to know about being brown, where he had been, and where we were. And there was Nathan's crew, hailing from everywhere and regarding each other as the family of their choosing, having left to get away from somewhere or having come to find something.

For those of you who feel like you've not quite happened upon your people, the more you are your true self, treat yourself and others with compassion and comprehension, and engage in that which feeds your soul, the more you will encounter those who do the same.

So...cherish your journey mates.
Together you are writing each other's stories.

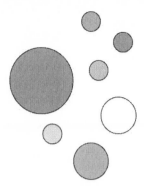

CHAPTER 6

No Matter Where You Are

O ctober 21, 2016 — I say to my boss, "this is going terribly wrong." She's a high-functioning, charismatic leader, who — through quite uncommon amounts of grit and ability to inspire others to act — has grown the organization from focusing on a few dozen people to impacting thousands.

We like each other a lot and by then communicate with a familiarity that goes beyond what one might find in traditional workplace relationships. And still, this is not an easy conversation. I fully expect it could end with my quitting or getting fired, though I don't know exactly how that will play out.

I tell her I want to explicitly run through updates on four priorities I'm working on, at a level of detail that's atypical given our roles. The gist is that the first two are going really well but are encompassing — releasing the

Android and iPhone app we've been building to our end users, and setting up that corporate / non-profit collaboration including relocating the entire staff to new office space. The third — reviewing some documentation and getting the lawyers to make updates — is fitting and starting. And the fourth — the audit — *I do not have a handle on*, so much so that I've gone incommunicado with the accounting firm.

For the first two, I want them to continue to thrive. The third, I want a driver who can focus on it. And for the fourth, I want it to fix. To somehow fix it. I don't quite say that I want to transfer them to somewhere I feel is safer. I also don't say that transferring them would allow me to offload the entire job — short-term or indefinitely — and get some time to regroup.

I tell her I don't know what's going on with me and that I don't believe I can continue to hold these things in my not okay state.

I am not my best 'self.' *I don't appear to be doing or being enough, can't tell where I'm supposed to be, and am sharing what's not yet sorted. I am not okay. I am surrounded by worry, almost hyperventilating, and forgetting things. I am scared of them because they are scared of us. Nowhere is safe, and the body I wear feels like a target. I run out of good times, tend in our suffering, and fight for the survival of home. I am beside myself with helplessness, neglecting and avoiding,*

112

and trying to push through. I want to scream, but I run out of words. I feel my insides, I'm getting cut into, and I am still running. I see everything almost burn down. I am over-tired and still going, until I scream for help.

We talk for a good while inside a space that is too merged professional and personal to tag as either. And though there is some unloading and the relative relief that comes with that, there isn't an offloading in the way I had imagined. I have not been fired, nor have I quit. There is only a thing to do next, and a hope that there will be some place clearer to go from there.

The only way out is through.

I am in the room for a long time by myself, working up the courage to do what I need to do. I look out of the twenty-third-floor window, onto the city. I pace, and rock back and forth on my heels. I am there, anxiously repeating these actions, until I conjure the nerve to take out my cell phone.

…I call the auditors.

I'm in the hole with my arms and legs thrust deep into the earth. I look up at how far away the opening is and lament the toil ahead of me. Then I find the courage and strength to slowly pull one hand out from its lodged place. I'm getting ready to start the climb.

Even though I had made the call and re-opened the lines of communication with the auditors, the next day, I am back in the office, still needing to face a dreaded email.

A couple of weeks before, I had emailed the contact at the external accounting firm to provide info and a timeline for the next update. And then she'd followed up the day after, then four days after that, then five days after that, and then once again after that. All with no response from me. The last email she had sent was sitting in my inbox unopened. I had seen it arrive but didn't have the heart to read it. Conjectures about what it said had remained on my mind all that day. It was the same day on which the finance call was scheduled. The email had hovered there unopened, weighing on my burdened brain — the same burdened brain that would miss the call.

I had met with my boss. I had called the auditors. I still have to read that email.

Have the courage to face that which scares you.

When I get to the office, I ask my right-hand staff person for an unorthodox, small, and enormous favor. "This is going to sound crazy, but please read this email and tell me what it says. I'm too scared to read it for myself."

You don't have to be courageous alone. Rely on your journey mates. They are in this with you, and sometimes can when you can't.

"Of course," he says, and thirty seconds later reports, "It's not that bad. It's what you think." He means it's a professionally written note stating the obvious. I have not been responding and they need to escalate the situation. I thank him, and then I read it for myself while my heart beats faster than it should.

This is me climbing out of the hole. This is me getting out of trouble.

With every vulnerable admission, every unorthodox favor I request, every task I complete, *I am climbing. I tell myself to reeeeeaach, dig deep, climb.*

I force my lips to form words, I push pass fumbling and umming, I get over how silly or out of my mind I might look or sound.

I am pushing through the insecurities, the physical sensations, and the narratives that might stop me from moving. I am going as soon as I am able to go.

Go. As soon as you can go, go.

Sometimes I even cross my eyes to make my vision fuzzy for a second before focusing on words I don't want to read. The time it takes for the blur to clear, providing just enough space for me to get okay with facing the words when they come into view.

I am doing whatever it takes, whatever I have to do to take care of myself.

I take deep breaths, I affirm that any doing is better than not doing, and after completing any task, I reward myself with an exhale and a, "Damn, that was hard."

And in these ways, I climb.

I respond to the email and promise to give an update on the audit progress to the accounting firm by the next Wednesday.

I make good on this.

Then, day-by-day, item-by-item, over the next several weeks, everything is turned in, and the audit report is finished. But, given the delays, the audit report is presented three months late.

All told, the financials themselves are fine. Revenue is up and expenses are below budget. There is a year over year net assets increase, and the auditors issue an *unqualified opinion* — this is the kind of opinion organizations want — that the financial statements are correct.

There are a few months of reckoning around how the process went and some humbling conversations among organizational leadership. But, in the end, my career survives.

I climb.

With every difficulty cleared, the Universe reminds us that there is a path and a way back to it. No matter where you are, trust that there is a guiding Light. Find it and go in that direction until things get brighter.

I tend rigorously to my introcosm and microcosms. I open all my mail, paper and electronic. Pay all my bills, put some on auto-pay. I start to show up where I'm supposed to show up, celebrating good times and huddling together in tough ones. I try to listen when my friends tell me to stop.

The hair biopsy comes in. I do have Alopecia. I start to attend appointments where the dermatologist sticks needles in my scalp, and my hair starts to grow back.

The tests come back from the gynecologist. It is not cancer. I have multiple fibroids that had been small and dormant or slow growing for a long time. But over the last year or so, they'd gotten so big that they'd protruded my stomach to pregnancy proportions and had started to push on internal organs. I need to have major surgery to excise them. It requires an incision all the way across the mid-section and six weeks of recovery. But, I am healthy other-wise and expected to be okay.

After the fire, we turned in the insurance papers and work with the building contractors to get our house re-paired. And after a couple of months of living at a hotel, we move back in to our house.

My father stops traveling to work in West Virginia, and gets off those freezing scaffolds and out of those under-ground tunnels. He has long since gotten the boot off his car and is no longer mad about that particular thing. He's alive and well, but according to him, maybe still poor. I believe we are far richer than he thinks, materially and beyond.

I am far less concerned about being in the silent majority. I am not actually silent. I am a sayer of words, right in the center, not in the margins, conveying that which I believe to be the sometimes messy truth, hoping that we utilize our awareness of it to effect change.

I do tell my father that I take back my assertion that I'll do something great. Good enough will have to do. He says, "Okay. Fine."

I set a practice around checking in with myself to make sure I get to and stay okay. I pay attention to whether I have cleared my voicemails, have consistently responded to reach outs from family and friends, have set up regular doctors' appointments, and have met milestones on personal projects and am making progress toward intentions. Once a month, I ask myself how I'm doing and keep track. If I don't say, "Yes" to *are you okay* questions I've written down to ask myself, I have committed to stop on the road altogether and find another way.

I climb.

By August of 2017, when I'm being wheeled into surgery, looking up at the bright light on the ceiling of the operating room, counting backward, starting to drift into a deep sleep, and not sure what I'll find on the other side, I am okay.

I still have the macrocosms with which to contend. The outside world is there and I still have to operate within it.

Society is still inhospitable to my people. Black people are still getting shot, by community members and by the police. We are still under attack. This is the truth about being Black in America. It is the world outside of the hospital as I close my eyes, and it is the world I look into with open eyes when I am wheeled out of recovery.

I deal with what's outside by seeking to protect that which is within, my energy and my spirit. To control my angst and seek peace, I go on media gray out — no television news, national or local. I only read the headlines from one press outlet to keep distantly abreast of what's happening.

To calm my spirit, I reconcile through my faith that we are finite beings on this plane. The best we can do is live every day trying to work toward the good.

I come a long way with bringing myself together. Through internal pushes, prods, tugs, and pulls, I accept my place in the intersections. I decide to put up shelves (proverbially and literally), coming to peace with living where I am. This is where I must be whole. It is from inside these intersections that I witness, record, and report.

I climb.

Then, I pull the weight of myself over the lip of the hole, and with a mighty heave, I am out. I lay there on the ground for a while, resting. Then lift myself up. And stand. I am back on my feet. I start to walk slowly, measuring my steps, proceeding cautiously until I feel steady. I look around for a light that illuminates the path forward, ready to follow the dots whenever I start to feel them again.

Recognize Your Findings

Findings are what we discover as we travel and use to actualize our purposes and meet our callings. The maze is speckled with them, and they can be anywhere — between your dots or in troubled spots — and can be easy to see or easy to miss.

If you're in a messy, scary part of the maze — like falling in or climbing out of a hole — it's hard to notice a glimmer of precious metal peeking out from underneath the soil. And if you're in a wonderful, charmed part of the maze, it can be easy to mistake fool's gold for the real thing and miss out on that which is authentic.

Be present and open so that you're able to recognize what you are meant to find along the way. Findings might be the little things from which you draw energy or unparalleled experiences happened upon — getting a chance to sketch ballerinas like one of your artistic idols, or walking through a real-life labyrinth — or wisdom or insights gathered after looking back on the journey with reflection.

Or they can be what you and only you are meant to discover and offer to the world.

I believe one of my purposes is to be a sayer, to live within a myriad of circumstances and then to *say* what is often left unsaid, to *tell the stories* often left untold, so that people can hear. And in that way, be a witness to the human condition so that we might better aid each other in it.

One way I believe I'm called to say, is to write. I got my palm read in high school and the reader said I was a writer — much to the chagrin of my Muslim stepfather, who said he could have told me this. And ever since, I have believed it. Over the years, I have written thousands of words — 100-word poems, hundreds of pages of fiction and non-fiction, and thousands of pages in journals. (One journal is signed by the eminent Maya Angelou). But the vast majority of my writings have not made it beyond the circles closest to me...until now.

In 2016, when I began to feel unsettled, I started to journal frequently. I knew something was happening, but because I didn't know what it was, I just wanted to write it down. I wrote almost every day. I lived and wrote. I wrote when I

> *"You and you alone are the only person that can live the life that writes the story that you were meant to tell."*
>
> Kerry Washington

had a horrible day, when I fled out of the movie theater, when I wanted to scream, and when I was rendered speechless.

Then, when I had made it through and looked back over what I had written, there it was. A priceless finding. A story. One only I could tell. And I never would have found if I hadn't fallen.

So…recognize your findings. In the best of times, they are what make the journey worth it. In the most difficult times, they are the reason why.

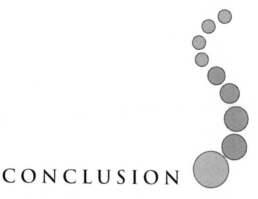

CONCLUSION

Remember to Follow the Dots

J*une 2020* - I finished my sojourn in March 2012, and by the end of that year was on a train back home to Baltimore. I was confident in myself and where I was headed. I wouldn't have guessed that four years later, I would experience such a crash — under the oppressive and enormous pressure of an unread email and a single missed meeting, which carried with them the weight of the world.

But, eh, that is how it goes. We make steady progress through the maze, proceeding with our best good peoples, and happening upon blissful alcoves. And then, when we're not paying attention, we realize we're lost.

We go through difficult times before we find our way back to the path. But just like it does for the heroine in *Labyrinth* — she rescues the baby from that magnificently stylish goblin king and grows into a better self in the process — life tends to work out. We find our way through the maze if we are intent on doing so.

I stayed in that executive role for two more years, including a move from leading operations to leading people practice. And at the top of 2020, I became a consultant for non-profits and socially vested for-profits to help organizations and individuals convert intentions into actualizations.

There have been many auspicious happenings since my fall and climb. I welcomed a nephew and grand cousin. I visited Alaska, Hong Kong, and Vietnam. And I had the privilege of sitting in the same chair in which the Good Reverend Dr. Martin Luther King once sat.

There has also been the worldwide COVID-19 pandemic, which has challenged our sense of security and how uncomfortable we are willing to make ourselves to protect the well-being of others.

Annnd…it appears the revolution has started, spawned by tragic and change-sparking occurrences around which have we have been incensed and galvanized. Ahmaud Arbery was killed by two armed white men during a jog. George Floyd was asphyxiated in broad daylight by a police officer while other officers did not stop him and onlookers recorded video. The nation has erupted into protests on a scale and with a consistency that has not been seen before by many, pushed forward by the names of too many people who have met similar fates. We won't take it anymore.

I am here for it.

Maybe in our lifetimes, my father, my sisters, my cousins, and my people might have access to the peaceable enjoyment of our bodies. And if not for us in this lifetime, we will keep each other company in this disquieted place, and push now for change that will come tomorrow, trusting that, "the arc of the moral universe is long, but it bends toward justice."[xix]

I am still in Baltimore, still in love, and still a proponent of the movements. I'm still very much aware of climate change, but instead of tripping out, I focus on what I can do to make a difference.

I am no longer on media gray out. I am finding ways to keep abreast of the most important happenings without letting the in-feed become overwhelming. I preserve the energy to get into the discourse and the action, to be a part of the change. I look for how I might best leverage my voice toward the future we want to see.

My hair has grown out into a Pandemic Fro. I wear big dangling earrings (on video call) to demonstrate that it's okay to do so, stand low to the ground at 5'1, and speak with a scratchy voice.

I am intent on giving air to the multivariate nature of our stories.

I am still making peace with the hardships, and seeking the calm, clarity, and joy.

I am still looking to keep to the path.

I am still trying to be the soul I intend to be in the midst of the world, so that when it comes time for me to try to pass through to the next plane, I make it.

I am still following the dots.

Beyond what I've shared thus far, here are some additional insights gathered as I've traveled:

Everything is all mixed in. Though the stories I've shared are true, they are — of course — incomprehensibly incomplete. It's impossible to speak of everything that happens within a single minute of any single day of any human life, never mind what has happened over the span of a couple months or a couple of years.

Though my trip to Barcelona was disproportionately positive, I definitely experienced some knocks and pangs during the trip. On a street corner in Mallorca, there were a few minutes when my girlfriends and I wanted to strangle each other — we were hung over and stepping right on each other's last nerves. And when I got to the end of my trip, I knew I had missed out on what could have been quite a lovely love affair.

And though my falling into a breakdown was disproportionately painful, there were definitely wins and upsides throughout that time. I got to play, riding a monster truck over sand dunes at the Jersey Shore. I had been there to watch and cheer as my father, brother, and husband had the once-in-a-lifetime experience of jumping out of a plane all together. And, I also won a longstanding battle with a habit that did not serve me. I am now a recovering procrastinator and I'm very pleased to say, I stay on top of things one day at a time.

There's no part of the road that's 100% mess or 100% charm. Life's tragic and wonderful experiences are all mixed in and have their place. It is a beautiful struggle where we look to have more auspicious times than not, hope to find solace in the sadness, and where we trust that even with the mix, all things are working toward good.

Take stock of where you *really* are. When the news of the house fire spread through my community of friends, they instinctively called to check on me. I distinctly remember talking with one friend and explaining that with all the things that had been going on, and all the ways I had been feeling, the fire, *actually*, had been an upside. You see, my house had *almost* burned down, but it had not. I knew right when it happened, that it was a blessing. The fire had granted me a clear and unequivocal chance to recognize and acknowledge all for which I had to be grateful.

You just might send in a rainbow for someone else. When I was in Rome having the time of my life, for a minute or two my arms were wrapped around a sobbing human who was having a very different experience. And, sometime in October 2016, when I was feeling relatively awful, I woke up to an email out of the blue with the subject line, "Love you" and the body reading only also, "Love you!" It was from a college friend, who I hadn't spoken to in years. Though at the time I was struggling to respond to anything quickly or at all, I responded right away. I told him I thought of him and how he greeted everyone with a kiss on the cheek. He was always so kind in times when it was not the norm to be so. I told him I loved him and that I hoped that my message reached him like his had reached me. I had barely made it through a storm of a day, and his message came in like a rainbow telling me it would be okay. You never know what a little love can do for a person in the times when they are most in need.

"This too shall pass."[xx] On my second day in Spain, I journaled: "One whole day in Barcelona already gone by. Sadness." I felt what I know is true for all things: they pass. When there's something awful, you can rest assured that it will not last forever. So make your way through, as it'll soon be gone. When there's something marvelous and magical, cherish it, because those moments do not last forever either.

I did not kiss the Englishman with deep blue eyes, but I should have. At the time, I was distracted by a fool's gold thing that had not even really begun until I had started my sojourn, and that fizzled out immediately after I arrived back in New York. I would meet my husband years later. And by way of the endless serendipity and confidence that we find within our love, I am sure we are where and with whom we're supposed to be. But, I'm also pretty sure I missed a dot on my way here. Be present in and fully embrace the moment, for all things pass, the bad and good alike.

Speak up even if your voice is shaking. Read "Listen to the Mustn'ts" and know that anything you want to be possible can be. Kiss the Englishman. Take your family on that cruise. Apologize. Make amends and reparations. And cherish the warm sun on your face before the sky returns to dusk. Some opportunities do not return. And there is a chance we only live but once.

So...

Go

As soon as you can, even if you're just on the underside of ready. Your next dot is often on the other side of fear.

Watch Out for Holes

The ones we dig for ourselves, the ones the world makes for us, and everything in between. And, if you find yourself in crisis, stop, call for help, and get ready to climb.

Feel for the Serenity

Look within and ask if you're steady, open, accepting, hopeful, grateful, present, and aware of grace. *Feel* for the calm, the clarity, and the joy. Look for the dots.

Feel for the Disruption

Recognize when you're in trouble. It is the time to pay the most attention, hear the messages, and look in the direction of the Light, so you can find your way out.

Cherish Your Journey Mates

Whether your journey mates come in the form of life-long partners and friends or passersby, who gift you exactly what you need but could not provide for yourself. Cherish them and be cherished among them. We are in this together.

Recognize Your Findings

Be present in the dark and Light times alike and recognize that which is being gifted. Use what you find to contribute to the good and you just might do something great. You'll most certainly do something that is *enough*. And who knows, your enough might be just in time for the revolution.

And, Remember to Follow the Dots.

If you're not sure you're on the right path, ask the Universe:

- Who am I?
- Where am I?
- Is this where I'm supposed to be?
- Is this who I'm supposed to be?

And then wait for the response. Is the Universe smiling? Are you?

With this printing, I can say I am standing on one of my dots today. Thank you, journey mates, for helping to get me here.

May we all live exemplary, exceptional, and ordinary yet extraordinary lives, full of beauty and wonder. May we all find our ways.

See you in 'nem streets.

And Godspeed on the journey.

END NOTES

---

[i] From *Are We a Nation* by Sweet Honey in the Rock, who appeared on the Equal Justice Initiatives' Juneteenth day of remembrance 19 June 2020, and brought the question front and center to be asked.

[ii] *Labyrinth*. Directed by Jim Henson, Lucas Films, 27 June 1986.

[iii] Here is the link to my *Ignite Baltimore 2018* "Are You On Your Dot?" speech. I would recommend viewing the five-minute video after you've finished this book because the talk has a spoiler. When you're ready, it can be found at https://www.youtube.com/watch?v=Ky9ZupKyH3E.

[iv] The idea of taking a gap-year in my 30s came from Asmahan Thompson, Stanford Class of 2000. She is one of the most infectiously positive and brilliant spirits I've encountered. At our ten-year college reunion, Asmahan was two years in to a "mini-retirement" from her career. She had set up her parent's house as a striking off point to continue to travel the world; she had already visited all seven continents before the end of her twenties and wanted to have more dedicated time to experience the things she wanted in life. I remember asking, "*How* did you do that?," and remarking that I couldn't. She said, "Yes, you can." And that all I needed to do was make a plan to do so, and do it. I believed her because she had, indeed, done it. About a year later, I had added enough money to my savings to take that gap year. And to anyone who asked me, "*How* did you do that?," I passed along Asmahan's inspiration. Here I acknowledge her for being a maven of the notion of "can"—the daring yet completely reachable destination of, "yes, you absolutely can."

[v] Some of the books which most salient in my memory—which sparked my imagination and an unwavering affinity for words—are *My Father's Dragon* by Ruth Stiles Gannett, *Green Eggs and Ham* by Dr. Seuss, and very many by Shel Silverstein, including *Where the Sidewalk Ends* and *The Missing Piece*. When my sister read *On Following the Dots*,

she said that the title reminded her of a Shel Silverstein title. I had not done this on purpose but liked the invocation, and said that maybe it was what we've now coined a Silversteinian slip.

vi The dearly departed Honorable Elijah E. Cummings, civil rights activist, and congressman, who represented Baltimore City and parts of Baltimore County in the U.S. House of Representatives. He is famously known for often saying, to combat actions or lack of action that perpetuated human suffering and social inequities, "we can do better." We can.

vii When Tupac was assassinated on September 13, 1996, I was 18 years old. I remember the great loss I felt when I heard. Through his music and interviews, which illuminated a depth of spirit, an unfettered radicalism, and unapologetic and poetic willingness to say just about anything, he was the voice of a generation, calling to attention the truth of our experience in a way that could not be ignored.

viii A street in Baltimore. If you know it, you know it.

ix From the 1993 movie *CB4* and re-popularized in 2016 by *Eveylyn from the Internets* in her genius and hysterical video effusing platitudes for Beyoncé's *Lemonade*: (https://www.youtube.com/watch?v=3NI3ZjcLbe8)

In related news, Beyoncé had also "turned Black" around that same time, as reported by *Saturday Night Live*.

x Paraphrased excerpts from the placards in the Museu Picasso, located in Barcelona, Spain.

xi Gilbert, Elizabeth. *Eat, Pray, Love: One Woman's Search for Everything Across Italy, India and Indonesia.* New York : Penguin Books. Originally published: February 16, 2006.

[xii] Spank Rock, *Everything is Boring and Everyone is a F**ing Liar*, Bad Blood Records, September 2011.

[xiii] This is the actual picture of the tallat.

[xiv] The popular HBO Series, *The Wire* (2002 – 2008), was set in Baltimore and about crime, drugs, police, and education. Public case records of Bodie Barksdale were used to build key composite characters on the show. This made Uncle Bodie transition to being a little bit more famous than infamous, when it had previously been the other way around. He remained just as charming as he had ever been.

[xv] BBC News. August 19, 2016. *Nice Attacks: What we know about the Bastille Day killings.* https://www.bbc.com/news/world-europe-36801671

[xvi] Toni Morrison spoke of the "white gaze" and how writers who are racialized as Black sometimes are restricted by being sentient of the presence of an outside audience to whom they explain things one would not explain to Black folk. The liberation, she says, is not being concerned. It is impossible to translate the power and eloquence of Morrison, so you should hear her thoughts on the subject directly at https://youtu.be/SHHHL31bFPA.

[xvii] The galaxy of thoughts and feelings we have about and within ourselves. When I was looking for a term that encapsulated all that swirls around inside of us, I searched for "introcosm" wondering if it was already out there and defined and found this Twitter post by Steven Kotler, and then applied an expanded meaning of the term.

https://twitter.com/steven_kotler/status/816252277103149056

[xviii] The poem "Listen to the Musn'ts" can be found in Shel Silverstein's *Falling Up*, and inspires me to think beyond perceived boundaries and know that anything is possible.

[xix] Martin Luther King, Jr., popularized by our forever President, Barack Obama.

[xx] It's hard to confirm the true origins of the widely known phrase, "This too Shall Pass." When I first heard it, I was told that it was from the Bible, but upon further investigation, it seems it may not be. Corinthians 4: 17-18, captures the essence but does not contain the words themselves. *For our present troubles won't last very long. Yet they produce for us a glory that vastly outweighs them and will last forever. So we don't look at the troubles we see now; rather, we fix our gaze on things that cannot be seen. For the things we see now will soon be gone, but the things we cannot see will last forever.* Other, various sources attribute it everywhere—as a proverb from a medieval Levent around 1200AD, derived from a Sufi tale of an ambiguous monarch in the East, from Persian Sufi poems, from part of a Yiddish tale, from King Solomon, etc. *So,* I will attribute it to my grandmother Patsy P., from whom I heard it first. It is a knowing that guides my life.